Inseparable

WHO I AM, WAS, AND WILL BE IN CHRIST

ASHLEY LINNE

THOMAS NELSON
Since 1798

NASHVILLE   DALLAS   MEXICO CITY   RIO DE JANEIRO

Published in Nashville, Tennessee, by Thomas Nelson. Thomas Nelson is a registered trademark of HarperCollins Christian Publishing.

Page design and layout: Crosslin Creative

Thomas Nelson, titles may be purchased in bulk for educational, business, fund-raising, or sales promotional use. For information, please e-mail SpecialMarkets@ ThomasNelson.com.

9781401680237

Printed in the United States of America

14 15 16 17 18 [RRD] 6 5 4 3 2 1

For Maddy.

... when you are joined with the Lord, you become
one spirit with Him.

—1 Corinthians 6:17

Contents

How to Use This Book

When I was a teen, a pastor once said, "When you study the Bible, you're spending time getting to know a person, not just reading a book." His words impacted me greatly and made the prospect of studying the Bible that much more appealing, although at the time I didn't feel as though I had what I needed to really understand God's Word. Throughout this book I'm going to give you opportunities to dig into Scripture and use some tools to help you discover what God is saying. However, I believe there is so much value in simply reading Scripture and allowing the Holy Spirit to speak to us. I know we're all at different places along our journey, so don't be afraid to take things a few steps further if you want or to just interact with the suggestions provided. The point here is to love God more, and we do that by getting to know Him better—and we do *that* by getting to know His Word.

I use *The Voice* translation throughout and have added those scriptures to provide a more streamlined experience for you. I would suggest that you read the entire book of Romans in one sitting sometime this week in your favorite translation, but also consider reading through it in one sitting in *The Voice* for a fresh perspective. If reading it in one sitting seems a little intimidating, you can break it up and read two or three chapters at a time. If you've never read an entire chapter of the Bible, let alone an entire book, I promise it will change your life and be well worth the time you put into it! I pray that you will find the courage to give it a shot (see the appendix for a suggested Romans reading plan that will help you read the whole book in seven days). While we won't go through Romans verse by verse, the principles found in the book of Romans are foundational to this book, and I know you will appreciate getting the big picture by reading through it before we begin.

In each chapter, we will discuss an aspect of our identity in Christ and then take a look at different characters in Scripture as examples of those aspects. Following the character studies, you'll find an interactive portion of Scripture called "Step into the Story." Finally, you'll find "Come Together" discussion questions for you and a friend as you go through the book together.

If you've never studied the Bible before, I hope to guide you through Scripture in ways that are understandable and straightforward for you. But I also deeply desire for you to be able to read, study, and understand Scripture on your own. Our lives will change as we allow the Holy Spirit to bring the Word to life within us. The reality is that some of us don't have large amounts of uninterrupted time to read and study the Bible, so I want to encourage you to do what you can with what you've got right now. Maybe you only have a ten-minute commute on the train to sink into study, or just thirty minutes while the baby is napping. Or maybe you're on the other end of the spectrum; you find yourself with too much free time and want to spend several minutes or maybe an hour or two investing in something that has eternal value. Reading, studying, and living out Scripture is something we all can do. This isn't a competition to see who can memorize the most verses or spend the most hours in Bible study. That isn't what pleases God. What pleases God is our coming to Him in faith that He loves us and wants to interact with us. And I promise you—even a little bit of time spent in God's Word can change your life. It may be just a very slight, almost unnoticeable change. But it will be change, and even the slightest adjustment in your walk with Him can set the course of your life.

This is what the "Step into the Story" sections will offer you—opportunities to spend as much time as you can in God's Word. I'll provide you with a portion of Romans that expounds the aspect of identity we've

discussed in that chapter. This is where I will offer what I call "fluid study elements," which look like this:

Prayer: Always start with prayer. Ask the Holy Spirit to illuminate the Word as you read and to till the soil of your heart and prepare you for what He has in store. As you read, praying through Scripture and interacting with God about what He has said will change your life—I promise! (For a great resource on how to pray through Scripture, check out *Praying God's Word* by Beth Moore.)

Big Picture: Whenever possible, study what the entire Bible has to say. It takes more time that way, but getting the whole story is very important. I would recommend you read through the entire Bible at least once in your lifetime, if not once a year. There are dozens of great reading plans out there that can help you read through in just about any time period (check out the appendix for a good suggestion). Many Bibles have a cross-reference feature that will point you to other relevant passages of Scripture. Cross-referencing can be quite helpful in seeing how God speaks on a certain topic across the board. Being familiar with the grand narrative of the Bible will help you discern truth from error throughout life, and you'll be able to connect the dots much more quickly as you study the Bible.

Context: Just as having the big picture of the whole Bible is important, it's also important to remember that God inspired human beings to pen His Word. Each writer had a unique style, and being familiar with the flow of that writing can help you as you study. We want to look at the context of not only a particular passage within a book, but the way that passage fits into the Bible as a whole. As you're experiencing a portion of Scripture, it is helpful to ask, "Who?," "What?," "When?," "Where?," and "Why?" Whenever possible, read through the entire book, or at the very least, a complete thought or paragraph. (Many Bibles have some sort of heading or paragraph system.)

Original Audience: What did this section of Scripture mean to the original hearers? You can spend hours researching historical context and what was going on in the world for them. Study Bibles often provide historical context in the introductions to books of the Bible or through study notes. Many also provide word studies, commentary, or insights into the original languages. I encourage you to check out free online study tools, such as www.blueletterbible.org and www.mystudybible.com, and Bible software such as Logos Bible Software (www.logos.com).

Standout Moments: Make note of passages, verses, words, or phrases that stand out to you—even if they are verses or phrases that you don't particularly like. God speaks volumes to us through His Word when we are making ourselves available to listen. Additionally, we must be doers of the Word and not merely hearers (James 1:22 NKJV). If we fail to put into practice what God asks of us, we will be missing out on the fullness of life God has for us and forfeit knowing who we really are in Christ. Be sure to take note of what God might be asking you to do in response to His Word, and follow through in obedience.

You can weave through these elements in just about any order, as many times as you need to as you go through a portion of Scripture. I'll provide a few passages for you on the pages here, but the sky is the limit for you as you interact with God through the Word. I suggest having a notebook of some sort handy to make notes as you study, whether that's your journal, a tablet, or a sketch pad. Don't be afraid to use highlighters, colored pencils, or even crayons to help you visualize and solidify concepts.

One of the many awesome things about Scripture and having such a creative God is that as we soak in His presence, we often find ourselves needing some kind of outlet for what He is doing in us. And of course, creativity looks different for everyone. So, write a song; paint a picture; bake a cake; build a model car; take a friend to lunch; volunteer at a community organization; do whatever it is that gets you going in response to His Word. In short, do something to worship Him. Act on what He's telling you!

And finally, be sure to share your experiences with others. Each chapter will wrap up with discussion questions for you to use with a friend or small group. If you don't have someone nearby that you can meet with physically, there is always the Internet; I'm sure you could find a few folks via our InScribed Facebook page (www.facebook.com/inscribedstudies)! Read the portions of Scripture you'll find in the "Step into the Story" sections and share with each other what you learned through the "Come Together" questions. Be sure to spend time in prayer together as well. You can decide together how quickly or slowly you want to go through this book; a chapter a week may be perfect for your crew, or a chapter every other week may better suit you. However long it takes and whatever that community looks like for you, dig in together and watch what happens.

I'm praying that God steadily transforms us all into Christ's likeness as we realize who we really are and become more of who He has made us to be.

CHAPTER ONE

IN Christ

A few nights ago, I was lying in bed, praying about this book, as I have done many, many nights previous. It feels as if I've been praying about this book for years—and that I've been asking God who I am for even longer. Finally, I feel He has answered me clearly. That night, as I was nestled safely in my bed, He lovingly whispered, *"It doesn't matter who you are. I AM."*

For a book about my identity in Christ, what matters most in that sentence is "Christ." The truth is, no matter who I am, Christ is the same today as He was yesterday and a thousand years before that. He *is*. He is God. He is the One who walked on water, who raised the dead, who spoke through prophets, who spoke the very universe into existence. And I am a very, very miniscule part of that universe. In ten thousand years it won't matter who I am. What will matter is who God is.

But even though I am merely a speck of dust in this vast expanse, God undeniably cares for me. I don't know that I'll ever really understand how or why. Maybe that's okay.

If He cares for me, He cares for you and billions upon billions of other people too. If He spent an incomprehensible number of years creating His divine rescue plan and executing that plan through His Son at just the right moment, I have to believe that it wasn't for nothing. He wouldn't do that for a bunch of meaningless dust. He would do it for something He cherishes, for creations that somehow matter, even if they are small in the grand scheme of things. He would do that for the beings He intended to bear His likeness.

I've come to realize that if I'm truly in Christ and allowing Him to shape me into His image, then I have to stop trying to "put Jesus first" in my life. In the past, by attempting to prioritize Him, I was implying that there were arenas in my life into which He was not allowed. I wondered what it would look like to instead view myself as a sponge and Jesus as water. Or perhaps to look to Him as the wind in my sails and not as a copilot. Or even better, to see Jesus as the Master Artist, painting the whole of time and space, and me as the tiniest paintbrush available that He chooses to use.

I think I went through a lot of my life observing Jesus rather than being saturated in Him. I concentrated hard on knowing as much as I could about Jesus and the Bible and following the rules. I had faith that He had saved me and had a plan for my life. But it took a while for me to really trust Him (and honestly, it is something I continually work on). It took some time for me to stop dipping my toes in and just dive in deep. It also took a while for me to let Jesus define me. I had always called myself a Christian, but that was just my face to the world. What about the deepest parts of me? I had a really messed-up view of myself for a really long time, and I'm not just talking about a low self-esteem. I struggled to know why I was still alive, why I mattered at all to anybody

> I've come to realize that if I'm truly in Christ and allowing Him to shape me into His image, then I have to stop trying to "put Jesus first" in my life.

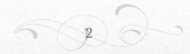

in the world, and what on earth God was thinking when He put me here. Did God really love me? A lot of really horrible things had happened to me, but I knew Jesus had suffered more than I ever had. I struggled with what it meant to not just say I was a Christian but to actually live as a disciple of Jesus even when no one was looking.

Being in Christ is a big deal. It's a make-it-or-break-it kind of deal. You're either in Christ or you aren't. Personally, I really would like to think that in the end everybody makes it to heaven. But if that were the case, why in the world would the Son of God go through torture and crucifixion? The fact of the matter is, "God loved the world in this way: He gave His One and Only Son, so that everyone who believes in Him will not perish but have eternal life" (John 3:16 HCSB). Jesus' message was, "Repent, for the kingdom of heaven is at hand" (Matt. 4:17 ESV). The word "repent" literally means to change one's mind or perception; to stop pursuing one direction of life, turn around, and go in a different direction. I pray that if you haven't already turned from sin to pursue Jesus, this book will help you do that. Following Christ, being in Christ, is the best adventure we could ever have because it is an eternal one, and it is worth any challenges we might face along the way.

I think it is interesting how sometimes we can base a lot of our beliefs on ideas that aren't really found in Scripture; ideas like "God won't give us more than we can handle" or "a penny saved is a penny earned." I'm certain I've been guilty of mistaking conventional wisdom for Scripture. So I really want to be sure that what we're talking about here is a concept that is biblical. What does it mean to be "in Christ"? Is this some concept people came up with, or is it scriptural? We have some pretty solid evidence from the words of Jesus Himself in John 14–17. Go ahead and read through these chapters now. Pay close attention to these verses:

> "If you love Me, obey the commandments I have given you. I will ask the Father to send you another Helper, *the Spirit of truth*, who will remain constantly with you. The world does not recognize the Spirit

of truth, because it does not know the Spirit and is unable to receive Him. But you do know the Spirit because He lives with you, and He will dwell in you. I will never abandon you like orphans; I will return to be with you. In a little while, the world will not see Me; but I will not vanish completely from your sight. Because I live, you will also live. At that time, you will know that I am in the Father, you are in Me, and I am in you. The one who loves Me will do the things I have commanded. My Father loves everyone who loves Me; and I will love you and reveal My heart, will, and nature to you." (John 14:15–21)

If we were sitting across the table from one another over coffee right now, I would be leaning forward and possibly even taking you by the hand because of the urgency of this truth. Jesus said the Spirit of truth will remain constantly with you, dwelling within you. The Holy Spirit within you, as someone in Christ, is completely and totally present with you at all times. He's always there, always speaking to you, guiding you in everyday choices, reminding you of the things you've read in Scripture, showing you the way through life. He's comforting you when the pain inside you feels as if it is seeping out of your pores, He's excited with you when you know you've done the right thing, He's empowering you with patience to get through the day. When you don't know what to pray, He prays for you. When you've royally messed up, He lets you know. When you're so lonely you want to give up, He's the voice that whispers to you to keep going. He is there with you, all the time. He isn't just with you in church on Sundays. He's with you as you're doing the dishes, chasing your kids, taking notes in class, or watching YouTube videos. He's always there.

Not only is God the Holy Spirit always there; He is the most important thing about you. He defines you. If you're anything like me, you've spent a whole lot of time trying to figure out who you are. I love taking personality inventories, those quizzes that tell me my strengths and weaknesses and what I should be when I grow up. I definitely think these tools are valuable but not as valuable as the identity God has given me. There have been too many moments in my life when I felt I had completely come to the end of myself—that I had exhausted every ounce of ability, energy, and sanity that I might have had. I've had moments when I felt completely broken and useless, as if my life would never amount to anything. There have been more times than I would like to admit when I've felt worthless. In those moments, the Holy Spirit within me was all that was holding me together, whether I realized it at the time or not. And through all this brokenness, at the end of myself I discovered God. I saw that if life was going to be worth living, it was going to have to be through His power and not my own—as if I'd had any power to begin with. I saw that if I was worth keeping alive, it had to be because of who He is, because from my vantage point I was not shaping up to be much of anything. I didn't understand at the time who I was to God, and that was okay. He had plans to show me just that.

> *I saw that if life was going to be worth living, it was going to have to be through His power and not my own.*

While I felt lost about who I was, others feel that they have a pretty good grip on who they are, but they still often feel as though something is missing. Maybe they've been Christians their whole lives, but deep down they wonder if there is supposed to be something more to it. Could our faith be summed up by a bunch of checklists of do's and don'ts? I sure hoped not, but I did spend many years wondering if I was good enough for God. I knew He had forgiven me, but I still messed up and was uncertain about how He viewed me in those moments. Was God continually disappointed with me for not living up to the fact that He had died to save me? Did He ever regret saving me? I got to the point where I felt that I *must* be missing something. Surely all the other Christians around me weren't plagued with these kinds of thoughts and questions. But as I started opening up about it, I found that almost everybody was struggling with the same thing. We knew we were saved from hell if we died, but we weren't quite sure what life was supposed to look like until then.

So if we are all in Christ, does that mean our lives should all look the same? Do we all have the same identity? At the core, I believe yes. Being in Christ evens the playing field; there isn't anyone who is better than anyone else, and no one sits higher than Jesus. Does this mean we're all cookie-cutter Christians assimilated into "the Borg" in some kind of universal consciousness, destined to a life of being just like everyone else? No, I don't think so. God is vast beyond our comprehension, and His beautiful, perfect characteristics are innumerable. As bearers of His image, we are each unique in our expressions of it. This multifaceted array of His glory leads us to appreciate each other and our differences when we're in Christ. But in Him we're united in ways we can't comprehend.

Like the rest of God's Word, Romans has threads of our identity in Christ woven throughout, which is why I have chosen to focus our study on this vital book. Romans is often viewed as containing such complex theology that its study should be reserved only for pastors or seminary students. But I disagree. Romans is indeed chock-full of intense discourse, but I firmly believe this beautiful book is meant for every one of us. Right in the middle of its sixteen chapters sits chapter 8, often regarded as a striking summary of the letter, or perhaps more appropriately, the spoke of the Romans wheel. I hope you'll take a few moments to pray and read through Romans 8 (provided in the following pages) now.

Romans 8

Romans 8 is one of the most powerful, mind-blowing chapters in the whole Bible for me, and the crux for everything we will explore in the pages to come. Let's take a look at the entire chapter together to get our journey under way. Again, if you're not used to reading this much Scripture in one sitting, feel free to take it slowly, but I really think you'll find yourself saying, "Wait—that's it?" by the time we reach the end!

As you read Romans 8, underline or highlight the portions that stand out to you the most—verses you like or dislike, words that jump out to you, concepts that puzzle you, sentences that move you. What might God be asking you to do in response to His words?

Prayer:

Father, thank You for the invaluable gift of Your Word. Thank You for loving us in ways we can't ignore. Help us to hear Your voice speaking to us clearly what You would have us to know, do, or experience. We love You and are in awe of your glory!

[vv. 1-4]

In Christ, I am made right.

[vv. 3-4]

In Christ, I am God's dwelling place.

¹ Therefore, now no condemnation awaits those who are living in Jesus the Anointed, *the Liberating King,* ² because when you live in the Anointed One, Jesus, *a new law takes effect. The law of the Spirit of life breathes into you and liberates you from the law of sin and death.* ³ God did something the law could never do. *You see, human flesh took its toll on God's law. In and of itself, the law is not weak; but* the flesh weakens it. So to condemn the sin that was *ruling* in the flesh, God sent His own Son, bearing the likeness of sinful flesh, as a sin offering. ⁴ Now we are able to live up to the justice demanded by the law. But that ability has not come from living by our fallen human nature; it has come because we walk according to the movement of the Spirit in our lives.

⁵ If you live your life animated by the flesh—*namely, your fallen, corrupt nature*—then your mind is focused on the matters of the flesh. But if you live your life animated by the Spirit—*namely, God's indwelling presence*—then your focus is on the work of the Spirit. ⁶ A mind focused on the flesh is doomed to death, but a mind focused on the Spirit will find full life and complete peace. ⁷ You see, a mind focused on the flesh is declaring war against God; it defies the authority of God's law and is incapable of following His path. ⁸ *So it is clear that* God takes no pleasure in those who live oriented to the flesh.

> **vv. 5–8**
> In Christ, I am fulfilled.

⁹ But you do not live in the flesh. You live in the Spirit, assuming, of course, that the Spirit of God lives inside of you. *The truth is that* anyone who does not have the Spirit of the Anointed living within does not belong to God. ¹⁰ If the Anointed One lives within you, even though the body is *as good as* dead because of *the effects of* sin, the Spirit is infusing you with life now that you are right with God. ¹¹ If the Spirit of the One who resurrected Jesus from the dead lives inside of you, then *you can be sure that* He who raised Him will cast *the light of* life into your mortal bodies through the life-giving power of the Spirit residing in you.

> **vv. 5–11**
> In Christ, I am alive.

¹² So, my brothers and sisters, you owe the flesh nothing! You do not need to live according to its ways, *so abandon its oppressive regime.* ¹³For if your life is just about satisfying the impulses of your sinful nature, then prepare to die. But if you have invited the Spirit to destroy these selfish desires, you will experience life. ¹⁴ If the Spirit of God is leading you, then *take comfort in knowing* you are His children.

> **vv. 12–14**
> In Christ, I am free.

¹⁵ You see, you have not received a spirit that returns you to slavery, so you have nothing to fear. The Spirit you have received adopts you *and welcomes you* into God's own family. That's why we call out to Him, "Abba! Father!" *as we would address a loving daddy.* ¹⁶ *Through that prayer,* God's Spirit confirms in our spirits that we are His children.

> **vv. 15–17**
> In Christ, I am part of a family.

¹⁷ If we are God's children, that means we are His heirs along with the Anointed, set to inherit everything that is His. If we share His sufferings, *we know that* we will ultimately share in His glory.

[18] Now I'm sure of this: the sufferings we endure now are not even worth comparing to the glory that is coming and will be revealed in us. [19] For all of creation is waiting, yearning for the time when the children of God will be revealed. [20] You see, all of creation has collapsed into emptiness, not by its own choosing, but by God's. Still He placed within it a *deep and abiding* hope [21] that creation would one day be liberated from its slavery to corruption and experience the glorious freedom of the children of God.

vv. 17–25

In Christ, I am an heir.

[22] For we know that all creation groans *in unison* with birthing pains up until now. [23] *And there is more;* it's not just creation—all of us are groaning together too. Though we have already tasted the firstfruits of the Spirit, we are longing for the total redemption of our bodies that comes when our adoption as children *of God* is complete—[24] for we have been saved in this hope *and for this future*. But hope does not involve what we already *have or* see. For who goes around hoping for what he already has? [25] But if we wait expectantly for things we have never seen, then we hope with true perseverance and eager anticipation.

[26] A similar thing happens *when we pray*. We are weak and do not know how to pray, so the Spirit steps in and articulates prayers for us with groaning too profound for words.

vv. 25–28

In Christ, I am commissioned.

[27] *Don't you know that* He who pursues and explores the human heart *intimately* knows the Spirit's mind because He pleads to God for His saints to align their lives with the will of God? [28] We are confident that God is able to orchestrate everything to work toward something good *and beautiful* when we love Him and accept His invitation to live according to His plan.

vv. 27–31

In Christ, I am avenged.

[29–30] *From the distant past, His eternal love reached into the future.* You see, He knew those who would be His one day, and He chose them beforehand to be conformed to the image of His Son so that Jesus would be the firstborn of a new family of believers, all brothers and sisters. As for those He chose beforehand, He called them to a different destiny so that they would experience what it means to be made right with God and share in His glory.

[31]So what should we say about all of this? If God is on our side, *then tell me:* whom should we fear? [32] If He did not spare His own Son,

but handed Him over on our account, then *don't you think that* He will graciously give us all things with Him? ³³ Can anyone be so bold as to level a charge against God's chosen? *Especially since* God's *"not guilty"* verdict is already declared. ³⁴ Who has the authority to condemn? Jesus the Anointed who died, but *more importantly, conquered death when He* was raised to sit at the right hand of God where He pleads on our behalf. ³⁵ So who can separate us? What can come between us and the love of God's Anointed? Can troubles, hardships, persecution, hunger, poverty, danger, or even death? *The answer is, absolutely nothing.* ³⁶ As the psalm says,

> On Your behalf, our lives are endangered constantly;
> we are like sheep awaiting slaughter.

³⁷ But no matter what comes, we will always taste victory through Him who loved us. ³⁸ For I have every confidence that nothing—not death, life, heavenly messengers, *dark* spirits, the present, the future, spiritual powers, ³⁹ height, depth, nor any created thing—can come between us and the love of God revealed in the Anointed, Jesus our Lord.

There is nothing that can ever separate us from His love. In Christ, we are inseparable.

---

vv. 31–37

In Christ, I am a victorious peacemaker.

Notes

New Creation

Therefore, if anyone is united with the Anointed One,
that person is a new creation. The old life is gone—and
see—a new life has begun!

—2 Corinthians 5:17

CHAPTER TWO

MADE

Right

What wondrous love is this, O my soul, O my soul!

What wondrous love is this, O my soul!

What wondrous love is this

That caused the Lord of bliss

To bear the dreadful curse for my soul, for my soul,

To bear the dreadful curse for my soul!

When I was sinking down, sinking down, sinking down,

When I was sinking down, sinking down,

When I was sinking down

Beneath God's righteous frown,

Christ laid aside His crown for my soul, for my soul,

Christ laid aside His crown for my soul.

—Christian folk hymn[1]

In Christ, I am … made right.

In Christ, you are . . . made right.

> Therefore, now no condemnation awaits those who are living in Jesus the Anointed, *the Liberating King,* because when you live in the Anointed One, Jesus, *a new law takes effect.* The law of the Spirit of life *breathes into you and* liberates you from the law of sin and death. God did something the law could never do. *You see, human flesh took its toll on God's law. In and of itself, the law is not weak; but* the flesh weakens it. So to condemn the sin that was *ruling* in the flesh, God sent His own Son, bearing the likeness of sinful flesh, as a sin offering. Now we are able to live up to the justice demanded by the law. But that ability has not come from living by our fallen human nature; it has come because we walk according to the movement of the Spirit in our lives. (Rom. 8:1–4)

In our journey to discovering who we are in Christ, we have to start at the beginning.

In the beginning, God created (Gen. 1:1).

Creation crescendoed to great heights, and the final masterpiece was woman. She was not a mere afterthought or a solution to Adam's problem. Did she solve his problem? Yes. She came on the scene and made everything complete. But she was in God's heart from the beginning. Male and female He created them—the perfect reflection of who He is (Gen. 1:27). It took both of them. Apart from each other they were merely dust. But together they were like a diamond, multifaceted and reflecting God's beauty and glory forever. And as if that weren't enough, He gave them the ability to reproduce that likeness through union and procreation. Absolute mystery and beauty walking on earth, that God the Creator imbued His creation with the ability to create. He could have easily gone on populating the earth making dust-people. But He chose to bring the creation into the story by giving them the ability and responsibility to go on creating, too.

And then it all just fell apart. Sin entered the world, bringing with it consequences that had never existed before: death and destruction, ripping apart the very fabric of the reality God had intended. Somewhere along the way Eve forgot who she was. In fact, she forgot who God was because somewhere in her heart she started thinking He was holding out on her. Check out the first verse of Genesis 3:

> Of all the wild creatures the Eternal God had created, the serpent was the craftiest.
>
> **Serpent** *(to the woman)*: Is it true that God has forbidden you to eat *fruits* from the trees of the garden?

Or, as some translations put it, "Did God *really* say . . . ?" Satan is like, "Hey . . . this God who made you to be so awesome doesn't really have your best interests at heart. He doesn't want you to know the whole deal here. He's keeping the truly good stuff from you. He's holding out on you. And you can't really trust Him. You need to take matters into your own hands."

Isn't this exactly how it goes so often with us, too?

Eve did take matters into her own hands. She ate the fruit. And as they say, the rest is history.

God covered Adam and Eve's shame in the first act of taking life that had ever occurred in all of time and space—He sacrificed another living being to make clothing to hide their nakedness (Gen. 3:21). But humanity had fallen . . . Eden was lost, evil had marred the once-perfect reality, and the world would never be the same. Death reigned and guilt prevailed. For the next many, many generations, the act of shame-covering continued to be played out over and over through animal sacrifices (Lev. 17:11). Until . . .

Jesus.

Sin entered the world, bringing with it consequences that had never existed before: death and destruction, ripping apart the very fabric of the reality God had intended.

Jesus absorbed God's anger against sin as the final, perfect sacrificial Lamb. He took the ultimate punishment and reversed our sentence. Jesus was tempted just as we all are, so He can relate to what it means to be human. But unlike us, He never sinned. "For our sake [God] made him to be sin who knew no sin, so that in him we might become the righteousness of God" (2 Cor. 5:21 ESV). It seems unfathomable: a completely innocent person taking the heat for something He didn't do. And He did it on such a massive scale that trying to wrap my mind around it makes my head hurt. Out of love for the Father and love for us, Jesus, God the Son in flesh, died an excruciating physical death and experienced ineffable disjointing of Himself at the core—separation from God the Father. Jesus gave everything of Himself so I could have everything of Him. Not just a "get out of hell free" card, but a destiny, an identity, a purpose, a brotherhood . . . a life.

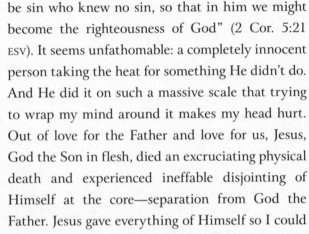

Jesus rose from the dead, vanquishing the power of sin and death.

Jesus rose from the dead, vanquishing the power of sin and death. He is alive, at work in our midst, and coming again. His Spirit dwelling within us continually chisels us into His image, lovingly working through us in this world gone mad. He means for us to live as "little Christs." Really. That's what the term "Christian" effectively meant when it was first used, most likely as an insult, way back in the first century (Acts 11:26). Today the term *Christian* carries all kinds of connotations, depending on your cultural definition. But regardless of what it may mean to other people, as followers of Jesus Christ we should be concerned with the biblical definition and look more and more like Him with each passing day . . . a picture of the reality of things unseen.

So how do we become Christians? How do we get back on course for what God intended for us—that close, intimate relationship with our Creator? It is simple but it is also costly.[2] We've already discussed the price Jesus paid; while the gift of salvation requires absolutely nothing from us except acceptance, there is still responsibility involved on our part. Jesus said, "Whoever does not carry his own cross and come after Me cannot be My disciple. For which one of you, when he wants to build a tower, does not first sit down and calculate the cost to see if he has enough to complete it? Otherwise, when he has laid a foundation and is not able to finish, all who observe it begin to ridicule him, saying, 'This man began to build and was not able to finish'" (Luke 14:27–30 NASB). We want to follow through as disciples of Jesus and not just as people who pay lip service, right?

This means we have to admit that we've been running our own lives and that we've not done well at all. We have to make a conscious decision to turn around and go the way God wants. That can be a pretty costly decision when you look at it from some perspectives—it can be scary to let go of control and put complete trust in a God we can't see. For some it may mean giving up friends, comforts, status symbols, or freedoms. In some parts of the world it means being willing to be killed. But the realness of life that comes with trusting Jesus is so, so worth any perceived risk we might have to take.

> So if you believe deep in your heart that God raised Jesus from the *pit of* death and if you voice your allegiance by confessing *the truth* that "Jesus is Lord," then you will be saved! Belief begins in the heart and leads to *a life that's* right with God; confession departs from our lips and brings *eternal* salvation. Because what Isaiah said *was true*: "The one who trusts in Him will not be disgraced." Remember that the Lord draws no distinction between Jew and non-Jew—He is Lord over all things, and He pours out His treasures on all who invoke His name because *as Scripture says*, "Everyone who calls on the name of the Lord will be saved."
>
> How can people invoke His name when they do not believe? How can they believe in Him when they have not heard? How can they hear if there is no one proclaiming Him? How can some give voice to the truth if they are not sent *by God*? As *Isaiah* said, "Ah, how beautiful the feet of those who declare the good news *of victory, of peace and liberation*." But some will hear the good news and refuse to submit

to the truth they hear. Isaiah *the prophet also* says, "Lord, who would ever believe it? Who would possibly accept what we've been told?" So faith proceeds from hearing, as we listen to the message about God's Anointed. (Rom. 10:9–17)

If you've ever wondered whether or not your eternal destiny is secure, you're not alone. When we sin, we may wonder if we've messed up beyond the point of return. If perhaps we have pushed God's grace a little too far. Many of us have this struggle even after we've decided to follow Christ. Let's go ahead and just clarify something off the bat here: I don't believe that Scripture teaches we can be separated from Him once we're in Christ. At some point, we must rest in the fact that our futures are secure in Him and that it has nothing to do with our earning it or paying God back for it. However, if we have a nagging, unrelenting sense that we aren't right with Him, it could indicate we need to reexamine ourselves and whether we have truly become His disciples. So, at the risk of sounding like a television evangelist, I do want to ask you as we go on this journey whether you are in Christ. Have you called out to Him? Handed over the reins of your life to Him? Have you voiced your allegiance to Him, as Romans 10:9–17 says?

> Because you, too, have heard the word of truth—the good news of your salvation—and because you believed *in the One who is truth*, your lives are marked with His seal. This is *none other than* the Holy Spirit who was promised as the guarantee toward the inheritance we are to receive when He frees and rescues all who belong to Him. To God be all praise and glory! (Eph. 1:13–14)

If you have decided to trust Jesus, you are in Him and He is in you. "I have been crucified with the Anointed One—I am no longer alive," the apostle Paul wrote, "but the Anointed is living in me; and whatever life I have left in this failing body I live by the faithfulness of God's Son, the One who loves me and gave His body *on the cross* for me" (Gal. 2:20). The Holy Spirit has marked you as belonging to Him. This is huge! You've heard the word of truth and embraced God's salvation. You are freed and rescued. And you belong to Him, branded with His seal so that you can't be separated from Him.

> You were once at odds *with God*, wicked in your ways and evil in your minds; but now He has reconciled you in His body—in His flesh through His death—so that He can present you to God holy, blameless, and *totally* free of imperfection as long as you stay planted in the faith. So don't venture away from what you have heard *and taken to heart*: the *living* hope of the good news that has been announced to all creation under heaven and has captured me, Paul, as its servant. (Col. 1:21–23)

Jesus has reconciled us to God. It's been done. There is no way we could ever make amends with God on our own, and we need to allow ourselves to enjoy the freedom that brings our souls. I hope you have felt the sweet relief of having the weight lifted off your shoulders through His forgiveness. Don't go back and pick up baggage you have already left behind. I pray that you will start to see yourself through God's eyes. When He looks at you, He no longer sees you as a sinner—He sees you as righteous in Jesus. Paul wrote, "Indeed, I count everything as loss because of the surpassing worth of knowing Christ Jesus my Lord. For his sake I have suffered the loss of all things and count them as rubbish, in order that I may gain Christ **and be found in him**, not having a righteousness of my own that comes from the law, but that which comes through faith in Christ" (Phil. 3:8–9 ESV, bold emphasis added). When God sees you, He sees the covering of Christ. Stay rooted in that.

Jesus has reconciled us to God. It's been done.

If you're reading all this and you still aren't sold on the need to be in Christ, I hope you'll hang with me through the rest of this book and see if you feel differently at the end. Maybe you are questioning your faith

and are seeking answers and truth. I desperately hope to provide you with truth in these pages. Perhaps at the end you'll still think all of us Christian folk are crazy. But I promise you, I will never stop praying for you or wanting to know your story. There are many, many things I believe about God, and a couple of them are these: (a) that God is so amazing and awesome that He's irresistible. If He's tugging on your heart, eventually you'll see Him for who He is and your life will never be the same; and (b) that God is passionate about you, but you can choose to tell Him no. He created us with the ability to choose to love Him back . . . or not. I don't like to think about the implications of choosing not to love Him, because if it breaks my heart, I can't fathom what it does to His. But still, the choice is yours.

Abraham

When it comes to being made right, we can look to Abraham as one of the very first examples of how God interacts with humanity and what God sees as important to restoring relationship. Abraham (Abram, before God changed his name) is considered a patriarch of the Jewish and Christian faiths. God called Abraham and made a covenant with him, promising him something far beyond just a huge family line. Abraham lived long before Moses received the Ten Commandments and other laws from God, so it wasn't his striving that made him right with God—it was his faith. Check out the account in Genesis 15:

> After these things the word of the Lord came to Abram in a vision: "Fear not, Abram, I am your shield; your reward shall be very great." But Abram said, "O Lord God, what will you give me, for I continue childless, and the heir of my house is Eliezer of Damascus?" And Abram said, "Behold, you have given me no offspring, and a member of my household will be my heir." And behold, the word of the Lord came to him: "This man shall not be your heir; your very own son shall be your heir." And he brought him outside and said, "Look toward heaven, and

number the stars, if you are able to number them." Then he said to him, "So shall your offspring be." And he believed the Lord, and he counted it to him as righteousness. (vv. 1–6 ESV)

It wasn't Abraham's good works or great lifestyle or adherence to the law that made him right with God. It was the fact that he believed God. Abraham took Him at His word, even though it defied logic. See, Abraham was well past his child-siring years. He had made arrangements for his estate to be passed on to Eliezer, who was perhaps a trusted servant, friend, or family member. But Eliezer wasn't his son. Abraham had done what he could with the hand he'd been dealt, but hope for a child seemed to have been lost long ago. Until that fateful night when the Creator of the Universe visited him and told him otherwise! Abraham decided to trust God, and that is what made him righteous. If you ever question what it takes to be right with God, remember that all it takes is faith. God is worthy of our trust, and that relationship-changing faith is what makes us "in Christ."

> *Abraham lived long before Moses received the Ten Commandments and other laws from God, so it wasn't his striving that made him right with God—it was his faith.*

You remember Abraham. Scripture tells us, "Abraham believed God *and trusted in His promises*, so God counted it to his favor as righteousness." Know this: people who trust in God are the true sons and daughters of Abraham. For it was foretold to us in the Scriptures that God would set the Gentile nations right by faith when He told Abraham, "I will bless all nations through you." So those who have faith *in Him* are blessed along with Abraham, our faithful ancestor. (Gal. 3:6–9)

Step into the Story

Before you jump into Romans 3, read Romans 1 and 2 in your Bible for context.

Romans 3

¹ So then, do the Jews have an advantage *over the other nations*? Does circumcision do anything for you? ² The answer is yes, in every way. To begin with, God spoke to and through the Jewish people. ³ But what if some *Jews* have been unfaithful? Does the fact that they abandoned their faith zero out God's faithfulness? ⁴ Absolutely not! If every person *on the planet* were a liar *and thief*, God would still be true. It stands written:

Whenever You speak, You are in the right.
When You come to judge, You will prevail.

⁵ If our perpetual injustice and corruption merely accentuate the purity of God's justice, what can we say? Is God unjust for unleashing His fury against us? (I am speaking from our limited human perspective.) ⁶ Again, absolutely not! If this were so, how could God stand as Judge over the world? ⁷ But if my lie serves only to point out God's truth and bring Him glory, then why am I being judged for my sin? ⁸ There are slanderous charges out there that we are saying things like, "Let's be as wicked as possible so that something good will come from it." Those malicious gossips will get what they deserve.

⁹ So what then? Are we Jews better off? Not at all. We have made it clear that people everywhere, Jews and non-Jews, are living under the power of sin.

vv. 8–9

CONTEXT:

Evidently there were those who were teaching that people could experience more of God's grace if they sinned more. This kind of logic contradicted all that the apostles had been teaching, and made no sense in light of the cross.

vv. 1–4

STANDOUT MOMENTS:

God is God. As such, He alone holds the right to judge, and He is always correct in those judgments. Additionally, God's faithfulness isn't influenced by anyone else's faithfulness. He is always exactly who He says He is.

¹⁰ Here's what Scripture says:

No one is righteous—not even one.

¹¹ There is no one who understands *the truth*;
no one is seeking after the *one True* God.
¹² All have turned away; together they've become worthless.
No one does good, not even one.
¹³ What comes out of their mouths is as foul as a rotting corpse;
their words stink of flattery.
Viper venom hides beneath their lips;
¹⁴ their mouths are full of curses, lies, and oppression.
¹⁵ Their feet race to *violence and* bloodshed;
¹⁶ destruction and trouble line the roads of their lives,
¹⁷ And they've never taken the road to peace.
¹⁸ You will never see the fear of God in their eyes.

¹⁹ We want to be clear that whatever the law says, it says to every-one who is under its authority. Its purpose is to muzzle every mouth, *to silence idle talk,* and to bring the whole world under the standard of God's justice. ²⁰ Therefore, doing what the law prescribes will not make anyone right in the eyes of God—*that's not its purpose*—but the law is capable of exposing the true nature of sin.

v. 20

BIG PICTURE:

Paul stated that the whole purpose for the law was to expose the true nature of sin rather than to simply be a list of things to do or not do. The law was given to shine a spotlight on humanity's need for a Savior. Even those who didn't know the law existed were still accountable to God, because of their ability to know right from wrong and because of all the other ways God had revealed Himself to them (see Romans 1:18–23).

²¹ But now *for the good news*: God's restorative justice has entered the world, independent of the law. Both the law and the prophets told us this day would come. ²² This redeeming justice comes through the faithfulness of Jesus, the Anointed One, *the Liberating King*, who makes salvation a reality for all who believe—without the slightest partiality. ²³ You see, all have sinned, and all their futile attempts to reach God in His glory fail. ²⁴ Yet they are now saved and set right by His free gift of grace through the redemption available only in Jesus the Anointed. ²⁵ When God set Him up to be the sacrifice—the seat of mercy where sins are atoned through faith—His blood became the demonstration of God's own restorative justice. All of this confirms His faithfulness *to the promise*, for over the course of human history God patiently held back as He dealt with the sins being committed. ²⁶ This expression of God's restorative justice displays in the present that He is just and righteous and that He makes right those who trust and commit themselves to Jesus.

vv. 21–26

PRAYER:

Lord, these verses bring tears of joy to my eyes! You have set me free, redeemed me, liberated me . . . when I least deserved it. Thank You, my God, for Your faithfulness to Your promises—promises You made thousands of years before I was born. I can't fathom what incredible things you have in store for us all as we walk with You.

²⁷ So is there any place left for boasting? No. It's been shut out completely. *And how?* By what sort of law? The law of works perhaps? No! By the law of faith. ²⁸ We hold that people are justified, *that is, made right with God* through faith, which has nothing to do with the deeds the law prescribes.

²⁹ Is God the God of the Jews only? *If He created all things, then doesn't that make Him* the God of all people? Jews and non-Jews, *insiders and outsiders alike*? Yes, He is also the God of all the outsiders. ³⁰ So since God is one, *there is one way for Jews and outsiders,* circumcised and uncircumcised, to be right with Him. That is the way of faith. ³¹ So are we trying to use faith to abolish the law? Absolutely not! In fact, we *now are free to* uphold the law *as God intended*.

Write down your own prayers and observations in your journal or notebook. Think about the following areas as you write (and check out the "How to Use This Book" section for reminders of what to look for in each section):

 PRAYER

 BIG PICTURE

 CONTEXT

 ORIGINAL AUDIENCE

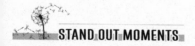 STAND OUT MOMENTS

Come Together

The gospel isn't just for us as individuals. The good news has implications for all of humanity and all of creation. God doesn't intend for any of us to follow Him by ourselves. Gather one or two friends together for this journey, and use the "Come Together" portions of each chapter as a springboard for your discussions. Read the portions of Scripture from the "Step into the Story" sections, and share what you learned. Be sure to spend time in prayer together as well, before you start and at other times as appropriate.

❋ What does it feel like when you know there's something keeping you from closeness with God?

❋ Have you ever struggled to allow God's grace to free you from guilt over something?

❋ Are there any areas of your life in which you may be trying to earn God's love?

❋ Share a "Standout Moment" from this chapter, and what you will do as a result.

Notes

CHAPTER THREE

CORPSE

Alive

From afar a light shines

Parched ground underneath

Cracks of dust reach further

Than I can see

Shards of clay surround

And fail to cut through the mire

The sun may shine

But not for me

Against me

Burning and burning

But I cannot feel anything anymore

Along the horizon

What shimmering madness

Is this

The gentle showers or

The coming storm to drown me

Dry bones dancing

If only for a moment

But wait

Suspended in air and time

Worlds tilt and gather

Is this

What it feels like

To breathe?

In Christ, I am ... alive.

In Christ, you are . . . alive.

If you live your life animated by the flesh—*namely, your fallen, corrupt nature*—then your mind is focused on the matters of the flesh. But if you live your life animated by the Spirit—*namely, God's indwelling presence*—then your focus is on the work of the Spirit. A mind focused on the flesh is doomed to death, but a mind focused on the Spirit will find full life and complete peace. You see, a mind focused on the flesh is declaring war against God; it defies the authority of God's law and is incapable of following His path. *So it is clear that* God takes no pleasure in those who live oriented to the flesh.

But you do not live in the flesh. You live in the Spirit, assuming, of course, that the Spirit of God lives inside of you. *The truth is that* anyone who does not have the Spirit of the Anointed living within does not belong to God. If the Anointed One lives within you, even though the body is as good as dead because of *the effects of* sin, the Spirit is infusing you with life now that you are right with God. If the Spirit of the One who resurrected Jesus from the dead lives inside of you, then *you can be sure that* He who raised Him will cast *the light of* life into your

mortal bodies through the life-giving power of the Spirit residing in you. (Rom. 8:5–11)

I have wanted to be dead. Numerous times. It's not something I'm proud of. It's not something I ever really wanted anyone to know. But it is true. Depression has haunted me from as far back as I can remember. As a child I learned to push down pain, sadness, and hurt because that was the only way I could cope with life. Only thing is, the pain didn't go away. It festered. It grew. It started to poison me. It leaked out when I was about sixteen . . .

I think I had casually mentioned to someone that I had contemplated driving my car over the mesa not far from my house. This kind of thought process seemed normal to me. I figured everyone had the same profound blackness in their lives. I got counseling briefly and tried some St. John's wort. It seemed to help a bit, and there were helpful things my therapist said to me that have stuck with me to this day.

> Depression has haunted me from as far back as I can remember.

But then I moved away for college and got caught up in other important activities. I never dug down far enough to really get to the bottom of the dark depths. So the poison kept slowly leaking into me. I had lived with it for so long but had learned at a young age that no one wants to really be around a depressed person, so I had gotten frighteningly good at putting on a brave face and going on with life—with school, with friends, even with ministry. I even fooled myself for a couple of years that I could live with the blackness and just work around it. It is miraculous and a total story of God's power that I have never actually attempted to take my own life. I didn't really want to muster the strength to do it, so I just prayed silently that it would happen somehow on its own. Death.

Fantasizing about death is no way to live. I mean, I lived . . . God even used me and worked through me in lots of ways in people's lives all around

the world during those dark years. He uses me still in times when the blackness threatens to overtake me again. Some would say that because I fight depression I don't have enough faith, because otherwise I would have been "totally healed" by now. Others would call me irresponsible for choosing to fight depression un-medicated; still others would call me faithless for the times when I did fight depression with pharmaceuticals. But one thing they can't call me is dead.

I'll never forget the first time I saw a dead body. It was someone I didn't really know, and I was a child—probably seven years old. We were at a wake or memorial of some sort, and we were in a small room with the casket that held her body. I didn't really understand what was going on, and I thought she looked really strange, as if she had too much makeup on. I think I tried to touch her face, but an adult stopped me.

The next time I was around a dead body, it was my grandmother's. We lived within walking distance of her nursing home, and the day she passed I had been by to see her because we were pretty sure she wouldn't live much longer. I was twelve. I remember sitting in the chair next to her, as she lay in the bed asleep, hanging on to the last hours of life. I can't remember what I said to her, and obviously she didn't respond. When she started making strange noises and breathing heavy, I got scared and went to the nurse's station to tell the staff before I walked home. Later that day, as I was doing laundry, I got the call from my mom. Grandma was gone.

Some would say that because I fight depression I don't have enough faith, because otherwise I would have been "totally healed" by now.

I went back to the nursing home, where my mother was gathering Grandma's personal things from the room. When I walked into the room, Grandma's body was still there. It was very surreal. She looked totally like herself, as if she were sleeping.

I've been to several funerals since my grandmother's, so I've seen my share of bodies. But the one that will forever be etched in my mind is my dear childhood friend. I have attempted to erase from my mind what his body looked like, lying in that cold casket. I don't like remembering him that way. In fact, I prayed with more faith than had used in a long time that he would get up out of that casket and be alive again. Imagine how many people would have believed in Jesus if he had. But he didn't.

In general we like to avoid death, don't we? Most of us wouldn't say going to a funeral was the highlight of our week. While some of us may love shows about zombies, nobody actually ever wants to meet one. We take lots of precautions to be sure we don't end up dying. We get our cholesterol checked, try the current fad diet, and look both ways before we cross the street. But do we ever look beyond the physical world and consider whether our souls are dead?

We've established that we all have an intrinsic value having been made in the image of God. We were meant to be alive and never have any concept of death. But then sin entered the scene, and the first blood was shed. No matter what you believe about our sinful nature—whether you think we are born innocent until we make that first choice to sin or born already guilty—we've all got it. It's like a disease. It eats at us and makes us the walking dead until and unless we are covered with the blood of an acceptable sacrifice. Recall that God's intended reality did not include sin, death, or destruction. He hates sin and everything it brought into the world, and only Christ's blood can remove it. Our souls are dead and must be resuscitated, resurrected. They desperately need the breath of God breathed into them. Otherwise, they stay dead, long after their clay houses cease to breathe.

When we are without Christ, we are dead. How do we come to recognize we are dead inside? Only one who has been brought to life can tell another dead soul what it is like to be revived. Those souls can testify to the work that has brought them to life, but they cannot bring another soul to life. Only the Creator God has the power to do that.

When we view salvation as resurrection of the soul, it changes things. A soul that has been resuscitated can't help but look, feel, and live differently from the way it did before. The soul may not have all the right words to say or the right behaviors down pat. But there's something very noticeably and remarkably different about that person. "If the Spirit of him who raised Jesus from the dead dwells in you," wrote Paul, "he who raised Christ Jesus from the dead will also give life to your mortal bodies through his Spirit who dwells in you" (Rom. 8:11 ESV).

I still imagine what it would have been like if my friend had gotten up out of that coffin at his funeral, as I had prayed. It would have been all over world news. He would have had one heck of a story to tell. It's the same deal when any soul is brought to life. It's definitely a story worth telling.

Often our personal stories of being "brought to life" are treated as blasé or passed off as religious fanaticism. How do you think Christ would have us react to this?

We deal with an unseen, paradoxical reality every moment of our lives. We can tell the difference between living and nonliving physical bodies—that much we can see. But the inner person, the soul, the unseen—that is so much more difficult to wrap our minds around. How does something dead exist within something living? This is where so much of the mystery comes into play for me. Somehow, a dead soul can make a choice to receive God's life-giving sacrifice. The dead soul doesn't have the power in and of itself to come back to life—indeed, the person doesn't even know he or she's dead until God reveals it to him or her. But somehow that person reaches out, from that part of him or her that seems to remember that she's made in the image of the One True God, and meant for a relation-ship with Him. God breathes life into the person, and he or she is . . . alive. Not just slightly alive (*Princess Bride* fans, please tell me you're having a Miracle Max moment with me—"Mostly dead is slightly alive"). Fully and totally alive.

Read Genesis 2:7, where God breathed life into Adam:

> One day the Eternal God scooped dirt out of the ground, sculpted it into *the shape we call* human, breathed the breath that gives life into the nostrils of the human, and the human became a living soul.

Compare John 3:

> **"Jesus:** I tell you the truth, if someone does not experience water and Spirit birth, there's no chance he will make it into God's kingdom. *Like from like.* Whatever is born from flesh is flesh; whatever is born from Spirit is spirit. Don't be shocked by My words, *but I tell you the truth.* Even you, *an educated and respected man among your people,* must be reborn *by the Spirit to enter the kingdom of God.* The wind blows all around us as if it has a will of its own; we *feel and* hear it, but we do not understand where it has come from or where it will end up. Life in the Spirit is as if it were the wind of God." (vv. 5–8)

Check out the language there—we must be born again, born of the Spirit. We need new life breathed into us.

The Greek word for "spirit" is the same for "breath." When we boil it down, what makes us "in Christ" is the fact that we have HIS SPIRIT within us. The Holy Spirit brings us to life. This is a pretty different view of salvation from what I used to have. In the past, if you had asked me to explain how a person "gets saved," my explanation wouldn't have been much beyond needing to say a written prayer or repeat a few scripted phrases. But now I know that becoming alive, becoming "in Christ," is all about the heart—the complete person, including both mind and emo-tions—and nothing to do with ritual. It doesn't mean that all salvation experiences need to be super dramatic. Most aren't. But becoming a

follower of Jesus, becoming a disciple or learner of Him, is definitely something supernatural. We can't breathe life into the fallen souls within us. Only God can do that.

There are many of us who can't pinpoint a date and time when we came to life spiritually. I'm one of those folks. My mother remembers the day I came to her as a very young child and wanted to "ask Jesus into my heart." Throughout my childhood I had a very, very strong sense of God's presence and was quietly fascinated with anything that had to do with God, the Bible, and church. I not-so-quietly preached to whomever and whatever would listen (usually a nearby flock of birds) on the rock outside my grandparents' condo when I was about four. I remember throwing myself on God's mercy when I started high school at thirteen—I knew only one other person in the whole school and told God He would have to be my friend because I didn't have any others. There are countless other moments in my journey as a disciple and follower of Jesus when I reiterated my reliance on Him and my need for Him—my need for His forgiveness, His grace, His presence. But I can't tell you the time and place when His Spirit took up residence within me and brought me to life. My guess is that many of you can't recall that moment, either. So I ask you to hang in there with me through these pages as we define ourselves as being in Christ and all that it means, and know that, yes, you are saved. For those of you who do have that awesome moment in your lives when you know without a doubt that you encountered Jesus for the first life-changing time, I hope that experience is burned into your memory forever as you continue your journey.

> We must be born again, born of the Spirit. We need new life breathed into us.

So where do we go from here, and what comes next? It can be really easy to be preoccupied with our sinful nature even though we've been rescued from sin's ultimate consequences. It is true that we will struggle against temptation for the rest of our lives, and we'll explore that tension later on. But what bothers me is how often we continue to view ourselves *only* as sinners. Many of us have been taught that we are worms crawling in the muck, plucked out of it only because God put His hands on His hips and said, "Well, I *guess* I can save you." That's not at all what has happened. At our very core we were made in His image. Do we have an infuriatingly frustrating inclination toward sin that just doesn't seem to fully ever go away? Well, yeah. That's part of the deal with living in a fallen world and having gone our own way rather than His. But that doesn't mean we are completely worthless. There is intrinsic value in each and every living being. I think we want to believe this, and often say we do. If we're into evangelism and missions, we may even let it stretch to being a fact that "God so loved the *world*" (John 3:16 NKJV, emphasis added). But for some reason, once we've been saved, we rather like to keep harping on the fact that we're sinners without taking the additional step of moving into a life powered by the Spirit. I'm not saying we shouldn't be very aware of the fact that we are in a war with sin, and we indeed must continue to examine ourselves and choose God's ways over ours. But can we mature in our faith enough to go beyond identifying ourselves as merely sinners saved by grace and move forward to seeing ourselves as new creations, as something totally different than we once were (see 1 Peter 2:5–9)? We are no longer sinners, dead and decaying inside—we have life beyond our comprehension. Because of Jesus' life, death, and resurrection, God has declared us justified (Rom. 3:24), righteous (2 Cor. 5:21), holy and blameless (Col. 1:22). And all that we are, we are in Christ.

> *We are no longer sinners, dead and decaying inside—we have life beyond our comprehension.*

★ ★ ★

They never travel the path of peace;

> no justice is found where they have been.

They set a course down crooked roads;

> no one who follows their lead has a chance
> of knowing peace.

**People: That's why we can't make things
right;**

> good and true can't gain any ground on us.

We *look earnestly* for a bright spot, but there
isn't

> even a glimmer *of hope*; it's darkness all
> around.

We are left to stumble along, grabbing at
whatever seems solid,

> like the blind *finding their way down a strange
> and threatening street.*

In broad daylight—*when we should have sight*—
we stumble and fall as in the dark.

> We are already like the dead among those
> brimming with health.

We growl like bears and moan like doves.

> We hope *that maybe, just maybe,* it will all
> turn out right;

But it doesn't. We look for liberation, but it's
too far away.

For our wrongdoing *runs too deep* before You.

> Our sins stack up against us—sure
> evidence of our guilt.

For our offenses are always with us; *they are
insidious and lasting, as You know.*

Our guilt says it all. We know it, too.

We *took You for nothing, and* did just the
opposite of Your commands.

We broke our promises to You, ignored
and rejected You.

We hatched up schemes to oppress others and
rebel, to twist the truth *for our gain*

while presenting it as honest-to-God fact.

When justice calls, we turn it away.

Righteousness *knows to* keep its distance,

For truth stumbles in the public square,

and honesty is not allowed to enter.

There is no truth-telling anymore,

and anyone who tries to do right finds he
is the *next* target.

It's true. The Eternal One saw *it all*

and was understandably perturbed at the
absence of justice. (Isa. 59:8–15)

For better or worse, the way I grew up was pretty religious. It was ingrained into me to be a good person. Fear drove pretty much every decision I made in life. Fear of punishment. Fear of disappointing authority figures. Fear of God smiting me. Even though I now have a much more accurate view of God and the reasons to make good choices, guilt is a foe I battle at times. (For those who battle depression, you know what I mean when I say guilt tends to be depression's helpmate, don't you?) Guilt

can eat your life away. Scripture teaches us that a pricked conscience, or "godly sorrow/guilt," leads us to repentance and life (2 Cor. 7:10). Any other kind of guilt just steals from us and destroys us. So it makes sense that a lot of people would avoid guilt by trying to balance the scales with the good things they do, by blaming others, or by trying to deaden their consciences. None of these methods brings life.

If I'm honest with myself, the previous passage from Isaiah 59 describes where I've been. As verse 8 says, I've traveled paths that were strewn with injustice and thought I would never know peace. Verse 9 perfectly describes how I feel when I'm depressed: "That's why we can't make things right; good and true can't gain any ground on us. We look *earnestly* for a bright spot, but there isn't even a glimmer *of hope*; it's darkness all around." And verse 12 gives us a clue as to why: "Our wrongdoing runs too deep." Guilt can easily throw us into depression. If you're in Christ and feeling guilty, there is a life-giving purpose for it. We'll take a look at how God corrects us in the next chapter, but for now I pray that God will speak to you through the following scripture and show you that in Christ you don't have to carry the weight of guilt any longer.

> How should we respond to all of this? Is it good to persist in a life of sin so that grace may multiply even more? Absolutely not! How can we die to a life where sin ruled over us and then invite sin back into our lives? Did someone forget to tell you that when we were initiated into Jesus the Anointed through baptism's ceremonial washing, we entered into His death? Therefore, we were buried with Him through this baptism into death so that just as God the Father, in all His glory, resurrected the Anointed One, we, too, might walk *confidently out of the grave* into a new life. *To put it another way:* if we have been united with Him to share in a death like His, don't you understand that we will also share in His resurrection? We know this: whatever we used to be with our old sinful ways has been nailed to His cross. So our entire record of sin has been canceled, and we no longer have to bow down to sin's power. . . . So here is how to picture yourself now that you have been initiated into Jesus

the Anointed: you are dead to sin's power and influence, but you are alive to God's rule. (Rom. 6:1–6, 11)

"Whatever we used to be with our old sinful ways has been nailed to His cross" (Rom. 6:6). As someone with an inclination toward unnecessary guilt, I find this passage incredibly freeing. My old self, the part of me that was inclined toward nothing but sin, has been put to death in Christ. In my new life in Him, that dead part of me may try to make a comeback, so it is important to put it in its place daily and remember this instruction from Paul: "Offer your body to God as those who are alive from the dead, and devote the parts of your body to God as tools for justice *and goodness in this world*" (Rom. 6:13). When we're brought to life, we have unimaginable purpose for the rest of our lives, no matter how long or short they might be. God doesn't breathe new life into us just to leave us hanging out at a country club until heaven. As we'll explore later, God commissions us to important work in the meantime. So, if you're carrying around guilt over things you have done in the past (and I am so prone to it myself!), will you join me in praying for God to use our past mistakes "as tools for justice and goodness in this world"?

You are dead to sin's power and influence, but you are alive to God's rule.

As you begin to view yourself as alive in Christ, I want you to know you are deeply, deeply loved. You are worth loving because you're a creation of God. When you're in Christ, you've been made right with God. You don't have to live with the tyranny of satanic guilt anymore. You're free to live, really live. But if you aren't in Christ, there isn't a delicate way to say it: you face spiritual death—the continuation of your current spiritual deadness and beyond. And that scares me. It terrifies me that any one person on this planet would not have the opportunity to hear that there is a way out, there is forgiveness, there is peace, there is life. It is my prayer that you will be raised to life spiritually today if you haven't been

already, and that through the study of God's Word in the coming pages, you experience His life-giving breath.

Lazarus

I think we all are pretty familiar with the story of Jesus' raising Lazarus from the dead, but just in case, let's recap here (you can read the whole account in John 11). Lazarus was a dear friend of Jesus, and brother to Mary and Martha. The Gospels indicate that their family was close to Jesus, and they helped Him and His disciples in their ministry, probably providing food and shelter.

Lazarus came down with an illness, and his sisters sent word to Jesus, who was in a neighboring town. Now, this family knew Jesus performed miracles and was probably hoping that Jesus would just say the word from afar and Lazarus would be healed. But this isn't what happened at all. In fact, it wasn't until Lazarus had been in the tomb four days that Jesus arrived. Everyone had more or less given up at this point, but it was all part of God's bigger plan for His glory. Jesus proved Himself as Lord over death by calling Lazarus out of the grave.

Can you imagine the scene? We don't know how many people were present at the tomb, but I think at least a few of them thought Jesus was downright crazy. Lazarus had been dead for the better part of a week. I love the way the King James translates Martha's statement of the obvious in John 11:39, "Lord, by this time he stinketh." But that didn't faze Jesus. "He cried out with a loud voice, 'Lazarus, come forth.' The man who had died came forth, bound hand and foot with wrappings, and his face was wrapped around with a cloth. Jesus said to [those who were gathered], 'Unbind him, and let him go'" (John 11:43–44 NASB).

I think it is interesting that Lazarus needed help getting untangled from his grave clothes, and that Jesus asked the people around Him to help unbind Lazarus. I don't want to over-spiritualize this, but I think there is some possible application for us here. When Jesus raises our souls

from the dead, sometimes there are things about our old, dead life that are trying to hold us back. We need help getting untangled, and that's part of why our new lives are meant to be lived alongside other believers. We need to leave the things that wrapped us when we were dead where they belong—in the grave. We are in Christ now, and instead of grave clothes, we are tangled up in His grace, mercy, and redemption. We are alive.

Step into the Story

Romans 5

¹ Since we have been *acquitted and* made right through faith, we are able to experience *true and lasting* peace with God through our Lord Jesus, the Anointed One, *the Liberating King.* ² Jesus leads us into a place of *radical* grace where we are able to celebrate the hope of experiencing God's glory. ³ And that's not all. We also celebrate in seasons of suffering because we know that when we suffer we develop endurance, ⁴ which shapes our characters. When our characters are refined, we learn what it means to hope *and anticipate God's goodness.* ⁵ And hope will never fail to satisfy our deepest need because the Holy Spirit that was given to us has flooded our hearts with God's love.

⁶ When the time was right, the Anointed One died for all of us who were far from God, powerless, and weak. ⁷ Now it is rare to find someone willing to die for an upright person, although it's possible that someone may give up his life for one who is truly good. ⁸ But *think about this:* while we were wasting our lives in sin, God revealed His powerful love to us *in a tangible display*—the Anointed One died for us.

vv. 1–5

PRAYER:

Father, I praise You for making me new, whole, and at peace with You! Remind me of Your radical grace in the moments I feel faint, and remind me of Your power and might in the moments I am suffering. Help me to relish Your love flooding over me.

v. 6

STANDOUT MOMENTS:

"When the time was right . . ." God is never late in His work; He is never early, either.

vv. 9–11

BIG PICTURE:

God's grace extends to not only our pasts, but our futures. We've messed up before and we'll mess up again, but Jesus' blood covers all our sin—yesterday, today, and forever. We are inseparable from Him!

⁹ As a result, the blood of Jesus has made us right with God now, and certainly we will be rescued by Him from God's wrath *in the future*. ¹⁰ If we were in the heat of combat with God when His Son reconciled us by laying down His life, then how much more will we be saved by Jesus' *resurrection* life? ¹¹ In fact, we stand now reconciled *and at peace* with God. That's why we celebrate in God through our Lord Jesus, the Anointed.

¹² Consider this: sin entered our world through one man, *Adam;* and through sin, death followed *in hot pursuit*. Death spread rapidly to infect all people on the earth as they engaged in sin.

¹³ Before God gave the law, sin existed, *but there was no way to account for it*. Outside the law, how could anyone be charged and found guilty of sin? ¹⁴ Still, death plagued all humanity from Adam to Moses, even those whose sin was of a different sort than Adam's. *You see, in God's plan,* Adam was a prototype of the One who comes *to usher in a new day*.

vv. 12–14

CONTEXT:

Paul pointed out that there was a huge chunk of time that passed between Adam's and Moses' lives. Moses received the law hundreds of years after Adam and Eve left the garden, but anyone who had lived in the time between still lived under the reign of sin and death.

¹⁵ But the free gift of grace bears no resemblance to Adam's crime *that brings a death sentence to all of humanity; in fact, it is quite the opposite.* For if the one man's sin brings death to so many, how much more does the gift of God's *radical* grace extend to humanity since Jesus the Anointed offered His generous gift. ¹⁶ His free gift is nothing like the scourge of the first man's sin. The judgment that fell because of one false step brought condemnation, but the free gift following countless offenses results in a favorable verdict—not guilty. ¹⁷ If one man's sin brought a reign of death—*that's Adam's legacy*—how much more will those who receive grace in abundance and the free gift of redeeming justice reign in life by means of one other man—Jesus the Anointed.

¹⁸ So here is the result: as one man's sin brought about condemnation *and punishment* for all people, so one man's act of faithfulness makes all of us right with God and brings us to new life. ¹⁹ Just as through one man's *defiant* disobedience every one of us were made sinners, so through the *willing* obedience of the one man many of us will be made right.

> **vv. 15–19**
>
> ## BIG PICTURE:
>
> The concept of Jesus Christ as the "second Adam" is a theme for some awesome further study. What are some ways Jesus is like Adam, and what are some ways He is totally different?

²⁰ When the law came into the picture, sin grew and grew; but wherever sin grew and spread, God's grace was there in fuller, greater measure. *No matter how much sin crept in, there was always more grace.* ²¹ In the same way that sin reigned in the sphere of death, now grace reigns through God's restorative justice, *eclipsing death and* leading to eternal life through the Anointed One, Jesus our Lord, *the Liberating King.*

Write down your own prayers and observations in your journal or notebook. Think about the following areas as you write:

PRAYER

BIG PICTURE

CONTEXT

ORIGINAL AUDIENCE

STAND OUT MOMENTS

❀ When have you felt dead?

❀ When have you felt most alive?

❀ If you are in Christ, do you feel alive? Do you feel that you're really living life, and not only living it, but doing so "abundantly" (John 10:10 NKJV)?

❀ Tell the story of how you went from death to life.

❀ Share a "Standout Moment" from this chapter and what you will do as a result.

> ♦f the Anointed One lives within you, even though the body is *as good as* dead because of *the effects of* sin, the Spirit is infusing you with life now that you are right with God. If the Spirit of the One who resurrected Jesus from the dead lives inside of you, then *you can be sure that* He who raised Him will cast *the light of* life into your mortal bodies through the life-giving power of the Spirit residing in you.
>
> **—Romans 8:10–11**

Notes

CHAPTER FOUR

FAILURE *Commissioned*

A task without a vision makes a drudgery.

A vision without a task makes a visionary.

A task and a vision makes a missionary.

—George Deakin[1]

To get the far away vision is the only cure for the creeping blindness.

—Author unknown

In Christ, I am . . . commissioned.

In Christ, you are . . . on a mission.

But if we wait expectantly for things we have never seen, then we hope with true perseverance and eager anticipation.

A similar thing happens *when we pray*. We are weak and do not know how to pray, so the Spirit steps in and articulates prayers for

us with groaning too profound for words. *Don't you know that* He who pursues and explores the human heart intimately knows the Spirit's mind because He pleads to God for His saints to align their lives with the will of God? We are confident that God is able to orchestrate everything to work toward something good *and beautiful* when we love Him and accept His invitation to live according to His plan. (Rom. 8:25–28)

Failure. We loathe it. We fear it. We allow it to hang over us like a cloud, threatening to ruin our hopes and dreams. We dread it so much that sometimes we choose to sit safely in our comfortable lives, never daring to step out and pursue the great things to which God has called us. There is so much that I have never attempted because I feared I would fail. For example, as a child I loved writing stories, but as an adult I've abandoned it because I am too afraid someone will read what I write and hate it. I often have some unattainable definitions of success in my life, and I bow to the pressure before I even make an attempt.

I think sometimes we put a lot of pressure on ourselves as Christians. Perhaps we feel that we have to know everything, have all the right doctrine, make every conversation "spiritual," and be sure we have witnessed to five people this month. There may not be anything wrong with any of that; Christ does undeniably call us to good works (James 2:26). But for me, years of self-imposed stress made me feel like a constant failure as a Christian. Doing the things I was supposed to would never be enough to make me feel okay—I was in search of a perfection I could never achieve on my own strength. We've been trained by our culture to work for rewards and to avoid punishment. What does this do to us when it comes to "working for the Kingdom"? What does it do to our relationship with God?

 was in search of a perfection I could never achieve on my own strength.

Do we live as though He is an angry taskmaster? When we have a foundation based on grace, why do many of us think we have to keep "paying God back" for our salvation?

I'm not implying that once we are in Christ we have the freedom to just do as we please for the rest of our lives, never taking into account His plans for us, never striving toward Christlikeness. If we've truly experienced God and His grace and salvation, "good works" are going to flow increasingly more naturally from us (Eph. 2:10). But those good actions can never be the basis of our feeling right with God. We're right with God because Jesus is right with God, and we're in Jesus. We're filled with His Spirit; He resides within us, guiding and directing us minute by minute if we are listening. Following His voice in trust is what pleases Him.

> *I* realized that my sole responsibility was to be obedient to God, and the results were up to Him.

I found a lot of freedom several years ago when I was in training for spending a summer overseas. I was leading a team that would spend a few months immersed in Asian culture, making friends and sharing Jesus. During one of the evening sessions the speaker conveyed something I will never forget. Holding up a chain, he described each of us as links in a chain. Each person we would meet that summer was somewhere along his or her "chain" in being drawn to God, and we would be a link in that chain. For some people we would be the very first link, the first person to ever tell those individuals about Jesus. For others we would be the middle link, watering the seed of God's Word in their hearts. And for a few we would be the last link, having the honor of being there when they surrendered themselves to Christ. This imagery instantly released me from the pressure of having to perform for God or see people as projects. It freed me of the need for control I felt for the decisions of the people I would meet. It enabled me to shift the weight of responsibility to the right shoulders— God's. I realized that my sole responsibility was to be obedient to God, and the results were up to Him. Though I definitely had an important role to play, ultimately that role was very small. God would be glorified, and that was what mattered.

The Holy Spirit is constantly in communication with us, so we have ample opportunity to follow His lead. Will we miss some of what He's saying? Most likely. But that's where grace comes in. Making a habit of listening for God's voice takes time and practice. For some of us that time span may be days, but for others it may be years. The important thing is that we remember that in Christ, we can do what He asks of us. We can do it because we're in Him and He's in us. So if He's asking us to do something, we can do it because He will be the One powering us (Phil. 4:13).

★ ★ ★

When the Pharisees heard that He had silenced the Sadducees, they came together. And one of them, an expert in the law, asked a question to test Him: "Teacher, which command in the law is the greatest?"

He said to him, "Love the Lord your God with all your heart, with all your soul, and with all your mind. This is the greatest and most important command. The second is like it: Love your neighbor as yourself. All the Law and the Prophets depend on these two commands." (Matt. 22:34-40 HCSB).

What is God's will? God's will can be boiled down to this: love Him and love others. We can only do that in the Spirit's power. If we are allowing love to be the life force of every decision we make and everything we do, we will get better and better at hearing God's voice and following His specific will in different situations. It doesn't mean we will avoid failure; it means we will redefine success. If success means growing in our earnest love for God and increasing the natural outpouring of that love through obedience to Him, then fear of failure will disappear.

Out of our overarching purpose to love God and love others comes another crucial part of God's design for our lives: being and making disciples. Jesus said, "All authority in heaven and on earth has been given to me. Go therefore and make disciples of all nations, baptizing them in the name of the Father and of the Son and of the Holy Spirit, teaching them to observe all that I have commanded you. And behold, I am with you always, to the end of the age" (Matt. 28:18–20 ESV). If we love God with all that we are and all that we have, we're going to have a hard time not allowing that love to seep out of us, right? If we're in Christ and Christ is in us, His Spirit is going to invade our lives, and at some point the people around us are going to notice. Our love for Him is going to rearrange our priorities, affect the way we interact with every person we encounter, change the very way we see people. Our love for God is going to move us to love others more than we love our own comfort and perceived rights. We will begin to have a desire to lay our own lives down for others, to sacrifice and let go of possessions, attitudes, and mind-sets because doing so will benefit people other than ourselves (even if we don't see the results of our sacrifices this side of eternity). This is discipleship—allowing God's Spirit within us to make us more like Jesus and responding to His voice when He calls. And one of the major things He calls us to do is to replicate this discipleship process in others.

If success means growing in our earnest love for God and increasing the natural outpouring of that love through obedience to Him, then fear of failure will disappear.

Many of us may think, *Who, me? I'm a total _____. There's no way God would trust me with making disciples.* But making disciples *is* your job. It takes time and commitment to another person, and usually involves modeling spiritual disciplines, such as praying, studying Scripture, and so on. A crucial aspect of disciple-making is sharing the gospel. You may think, *Oh, I don't have the gift of evangelism.* But if you're in Christ, you really do:

Jesus: I am here speaking with all the authority of God, *who has commanded Me to give you this commission*: Go out and make disciples in all the nations. Ceremonially wash them through baptism in the name of the *triune God*: Father, Son, and Holy Spirit. Then disciple them. *Form them in the practices and postures that* I have taught you, and show them how to

follow the commands I have laid down for you. And I will be with you, day after day, to the end of the age. (Matt. 28:18–20)

Jesus: Listen: I am sending you out to be sheep among wolves. You must be as shrewd as serpents and as innocent as doves. You must be careful. You must be discerning. You must be on your guard. There will be men who try to hand you over to their town councils and have you flogged in their synagogues. Because of Me, naysayers and doubters will try to make an example out of you by trying you before rulers and kings. When this happens—*when you are arrested, dragged to court*—don't worry about what to say or how to say it. The words you should speak will be given to you. For at that moment, it will not be you speaking; it will be the Spirit of your Father speaking through you. (Matt. 10:16–20)

Remember, the Spirit of God is within you. That means that the more you follow His promptings, the more you'll know what to do and say in any given situation. (Hopefully you won't end up in court or prison for loving Jesus . . . but for a growing percentage of the world, being a Christian indeed can land you in jail.) The more you seek to love God and love others, the more "evangelizing" will come naturally to you. I used to think evangelizing meant I had to knock on strangers' doors and immediately tell them they were going to hell and needed to get saved. But the more I started allowing God to shape me, the more I stopped worrying about "saving people" and started to focus more on obeying God. Now, I'm definitely not saying that we should just let everyone go on their merry way and never care about their standing with Jesus. What I am saying is that as we continue to allow God to rearrange our lives after His heart, we will (a) realize that it is the Holy Spirit's job to convince people they need Him, and (b) cause some kind of reaction in people whether we want to or not. Sometimes that reaction is going to be negative. I really want people to

> The more you follow His promptings, the more you'll know what to do and say in any given situation.

like me. But the Spirit of God within me is going to rub some folks the wrong way. This isn't license for me to go around being a jerk. We're loving others, not out on a crusade, right? Will I at some points have to be painfully honest with the people I love? Yeah, I should hope so—I hope I love people enough to be honest with them. But I have to remember that it isn't my job to save people. That's God's job. It isn't my job to fight with people until they finally agree with me or write them off if they don't. It's my job to love them with words and actions, to pray that their response to the Holy Spirit within me is one of curiosity rather than repulsion, to pray that God would till the soil of their souls to be tender toward His truth and love, and to pray that I get to be a part of God's work in their lives.

There's an old video on YouTube that you should look up, titled "A Gift of a Bible."[2] Maybe you've seen it. Penn Jillette (of the comedy team Penn & Teller) tells a story of how, after one of his shows, a man gave him a Bible. Now, Penn is an atheist. But what he says in reaction to his exchange with the man is really profound for all of us who are in Christ:

> He was really kind, and nice, and sane . . . and then he gave me this Bible. And I've always said I don't respect people who don't proselytize. If you believe there could be people who are going to hell or not getting eternal life, and you think it's not really worth telling them this because it might make things socially awkward . . . how much do you have to hate somebody to not proselytize? How much do you have to hate somebody to believe that everlasting life is possible and not tell them that? . . . This guy was a really good guy. He was polite, and honest, and sane, and he cared enough about me to proselytize and give me a Bible.

Who might you need to love today?

Making disciples involves so much more than the initial evangelism. Discipleship is a lifelong process for each of us, and the gospel is still vital for us once we are Christians. When we are in Christ, we have dedicated ourselves to learning from Him and allowing Him to rearrange us and make us more like Him. To "disciple" another person may sound really intimidating, but I think that perhaps the word *mentoring* may also apply.

I define mentoring as a committed, growing discipleship relationship between two people for the purposes of both parties' spiritual and personal maturation, with a focus on the mentee's needs as primary and the goal being the mentee's preparation for mentoring others, who will mentor others. In many contexts the mentoring relationship may come to a close eventually. However, the mentor may always be involved in the mentee's life in some form or fashion, as the mentee becomes a mentor herself. It is the nature of discipleship to produce multiplication. (Remember our chain analogy?)

You may think you aren't qualified to disciple or mentor anyone. But all it really requires is that you be willing to invest your time and heart in someone who is just one step behind you. In my experience, this happens best in the context of a friendship that feels natural already and isn't forced or contrived. If you're young or feel inexperienced, you may be intimidated at the thought of leading anyone to Christ or helping a "younger" Christian in her walk. But there are lifelong friendships to be forged, ones that fly in the face of our culture's disposable, pseudo relationships that lack any sort of depth. You have a unique opportunity to change the course of history by investing in just one other person. I don't know about you, but that's something of which I want to be a part.

> You have a unique opportunity to change the course of history by investing in just one other person.

I'd like to speak to those of you who are considered baby boomers, part of the Silent Generation, and yes, even my fellow Gen Xers. The younger generations are looking for those who have gone before them in some aspect of life, who have made some mistakes and are willing to be honest about it so others can learn from them. Young people are drawn to people who are authentic, and they can see through "fake" in a nanosecond. Young adults want to be wanted. A young adult does not need someone who wants to make decisions for her, but instead someone who will take the time to teach her how to make the best decisions possible in everyday life. I think sometimes we worry that younger people are going to suck all the life out of us, when in fact they can replenish us in a relationship like the one I just described.

A few years ago, I created an online survey to see if I could get some feedback on different sorts of things people thirty-five and younger were looking for in a mentor. I collected responses entirely online via e-mail and Facebook and got a total of 335 responses. When asked to choose what sorts of activities they would like to do with a mentor, the top three responses were: "Have casual conversation" (90.3 percent); "Self-evaluation and improvement" (81 percent); and "Hold me accountable" (74 percent). The remaining responses (ranked in descending order) were "Pray," "Study the Bible," "Career and job coaching," and "Service projects." Several wrote in that they would like mentoring in the area of marriage and parenting, making academic choices, and just life in general. I think this shows that a mentoring relationship with a younger adult is not as intimidating as it might seem. And for any of us, no matter our age or how long we've walked with Christ, I hope we can find encouragement in the fact that all we need is to be one step ahead because it isn't about us anyway. We don't need to be perfect, know everything, or have it all together. We just need to be able to point others to the One who *is* perfect, knows everything, and has it all together.

In a recent article submitted to *The Blog* (from *Huffington Post*), titled "Why Generation Y Yuppies Are Unhappy,"[3] the author theorizes that many younger-generation people are miserable because they have very unrealistic expectations of life and success. Additionally, social media creates an even more inaccurate view of reality: people assume that what they see on Facebook represents reality when in fact it merely represents

> *We* just need to be able to point others to the One who *is* perfect, knows everything, and has it all together.

the reality people want to broadcast, and it may be very inflated. As such, many people compare their current realities with these aggrandized representations and are left feeling inadequate and depressed. I have a hunch that this is not an experience limited to those in their twenties.

Instead of comparing our worst days to someone else's best days, what if we instead focused on humbling ourselves and asking God to show us His plans for us? It seems simple, but isn't it difficult to do? It is for me. I get caught up in the comparison trap, and my day is down the tube. But seeking God's kingdom first always brings more satisfaction than wasting my time trying to keep up with everyone else.

You're not a failure. God sees the successful covering of Christ when He looks at you.

Loving God and loving others involves making disciples, and God gifts us and leads us to do His will in varying ways. When we decide to pursue God's will instead of our own, that is when true happiness comes to us. God's plans are for His glory, and we get to be a small part of that.

I hope that these great commandments free you up to dream. Chase after God's dreams for your life. His imagination is way bigger than ours.

> "But as the Scriptures say,
> No eye has ever seen and no ear has ever heard
> and it has never occurred to the human heart
> All the things God prepared for those who love Him" (1 Cor. 2:9).

You're not a failure. God sees the successful covering of Christ when He looks at you. He sees endless potential because you're His child that He loves. He doesn't see your potential in a cheesy, self-help kind of way either:

❖ "God chose us to be in a relationship with Him even before He laid out plans for this world; He wanted us to live holy lives

characterized by love, *free from sin,* and blameless before Him. He destined us to be adopted as His children through *the covenant* Jesus the Anointed *inaugurated in His sacrificial life.* This was His pleasure and His will *for us.*" (Eph. 1:4–5)

❧ "For we are the product of His hand, *heaven's poetry etched on lives,* created in the Anointed, Jesus, to accomplish the good works God arranged long ago." (Eph. 2:10)

God has in mind unique and possibly unusual things that only you can do, but you won't be able to do them apart from Him. There may be risk involved, but living out God's commission means finding His definition of success.

Peter

Do you have "that" person in your life—the one who always seems to remember every mistake you've ever made, no matter what you try to do about it? I imagine Peter could identify. He is best known for denying he knew Jesus. In my Sunday school experiences, Peter was often characterized as having suffered from open-mouth-insert-foot disease. But is this really his legacy?

Take another look at Peter. He definitely got one thing right:

❧ "[Jesus] said to them, 'But who do you say that I am?' Simon Peter replied, 'You are the Christ, the Son of the living God.'" (Matt. 16:15–16 ESV)

❧ "So Jesus said to the Twelve, 'Do you want to go away as well?' Simon Peter answered him, 'Lord, to whom shall we go? You have the words of eternal life, and we have believed, and have come to know, that you are the Holy One of God." (John 6:67–69 ESV).

And although we may be quick to judge him for taking his eyes off Jesus and sinking in the water, wasn't he the only one of the disciples brave enough to get out of the boat? (Matt. 14:22–33)

But there is the sad reality that Peter turned his back on Jesus while He was going through the most important time of His life.

Talk about failure.

What did Jesus do with Peter's failure? In His awe-inspiring way, Jesus not only forgave Peter but restored his dignity and gave him a task: to feed and tend His sheep (John 21:15–19). And while Peter was definitely still human and made future mistakes, he took that task seriously, and God did some pretty amazing things through him. Peter was the first to preach after the Holy Spirit fell at Pentecost (Acts 2:14–41), he performed several miracles (most notably, a woman's resurrection in Acts 9:36–43), and he witnessed Gentiles receiving the Holy Spirit (Acts 10). Peter's letters in the New Testament are rich with doctrine and encouragement to keep the faith and persevere through suffering. Tradition holds that Peter was eventually crucified in Rome under Nero's regime, and that he was crucified upside down, not counting himself worthy of dying the same way Jesus had.

Talk about a legacy.

None of us has messed up so badly or gone so far off the path that Jesus can't restore us, revive us, and commission us. In Christ, our legacy is entirely wrapped up in His glory.

Step into the Story

Romans 10

[1] My brothers and sisters, I pray *constantly* to God for the salvation of my people; it is the deep desire of my heart. [2] What I can say about them is that they are enthusiastic about God, but *that won't lead them to Him because* their zeal is not based on true knowledge. [3] In their ignorance about how God is working to make things right, they have been trying to establish their own right standing with God *through the law*. But they are not operating under God's saving, restorative justice. [4] You see, God's purpose for the law reaches its climax when the Anointed One arrives; now all who trust *in Him* can have their lives made right with God.

> **v. 4**
>
> **PRAYER:**
>
> Father, Your plans are truly amazing, and I continue to be in awe of how You work in this world. Thank You for not demanding any criteria, checklists, or prerequisites for being made right with You. Thank You for Your grace and the gift of faith!

[5] Moses *made this clear long ago when he* wrote about *what it takes to have* a right relationship with God based on the law: "The person devoted to the law's commands will live by them." [6] But a right relationship based on faith sounds like this: "Do not say to yourselves, 'Who will go up into heaven?'" (that is, to bring down the Anointed One), [7] "or, 'Who will go down into the abyss?'" (that is, to bring the Anointed One up from the dead). [8] But what does it actually say? "The word is near you, in your mouth and in your heart" (that is, the good news we *have been called to* preach to you). [9] So if you believe deep in your heart that God raised Jesus from the *pit of* death and if you voice your allegiance by confessing *the truth* that "Jesus is Lord," then you will be saved! [10] Belief begins in the heart and leads to *a life that's* right with God; confession departs from our lips and brings *eternal* salvation. [11] Because what Isaiah said *was true*: "The one who trusts in Him will not be disgraced." [12] Remember that the Lord draws no distinction between Jew and non-Jew—He is Lord over all things, and He pours out His

> **v. 11**
>
> **BIG PICTURE:**
>
> Check out Isaiah 28:16.

> **vv. 6–8**
>
> **BIG PICTURE:**
>
> These verses go back to Deuteronomy 30:12–14.

treasures on all who invoke His name ¹³ because *as Scripture says,* "Everyone who calls on the name of the Lord will be saved."

STANDOUT MOMENTS:

There are people in the world who have never even heard Jesus' name, let alone heard the gospel. Is there a particular person who comes to mind when you read this verse? A people group, language group, or country? To whom might God be calling you to "proclaim" the good news?

v. 13

BIG PICTURE:

Check out Joel 2:32.

¹⁴ How can people invoke His name when they do not believe? How can they believe in Him when they have not heard? How can they hear if there is no one proclaiming Him? ¹⁵ How can some give voice to the truth if they are not sent *by God?* As *Isaiah* said, "Ah, how beautiful the feet of those who declare the good news *of victory, of peace and liberation.*" ¹⁶ But some will hear the good news and refuse to submit to the truth they hear. Isaiah *the prophet also* says, "Lord, who would ever believe it? Who would possibly accept what we've been told?" ¹⁷ So faith proceeds from hearing, as we listen to the message about God's Anointed.

vv. 14–17

CONTEXT:

Though he always yearned for his fellow Jews to accept Jesus as Messiah, Paul considered his "mission field" to be anywhere Gentiles were. He lived and breathed the gospel, the message of Jesus' atoning death and resurrection.

[18] But let me ask this: have my people ever heard? Indeed, they have:

Yet from here to the ends of the earth, their voice has gone out;
the whole world has heard what they have to say.

[19] But again let me ask: did Israel *perhaps hear and* not understand all of this? *Well,* Moses was the first to say,

I will make you jealous with a people who are not a nation.
With a senseless people I will anger you.

[20] Then Isaiah the fearless *prophet* says it this way:

I was found by people who did not seek Me;
I showed My face to those who never asked for Me.

[21] And as to *the fate of* Israel, God says,

All day long I opened My hands
to a rebellious people, who constantly work against Me.

Write down your own prayers and observations in your journal or notebook. Think about the following areas as you write:

 **PRAYER**

 **BIG PICTURE**

 **CONTEXT**

 **ORIGINAL AUDIENCE**

 **STAND OUT MOMENTS**

Come Together

❖ When was a time you felt you had utterly failed? What did you do immediately following? How has it affected your life up to now?

❖ How would you define your dreams?

❖ Are you dreaming God's dreams for your life?

❖ In what ways are you currently making disciples? Where do you have room for improvement?

❖ What is God's will for your life in this moment? Is there anything specific you know He is asking you to do as you seek to align your life with loving Him and loving others?

❖ Share a "Standout Moment" from this chapter and what you will do as a result.

> Some want to live within the sound of the church or chapel bell;
>
> I want to run a rescue shop within a yard of hell.

—C. T. Studd (1860–1931)

Notes

As We Go

Cultivate *all* these practices; live by them so that all will
see *how* you are advancing *and growing*.

—1 Timothy 4:15

CHAPTER FIVE

Saint

"Before God, identity is not a both/and
(sinner *and* righteous); it is an either/or
(sinner *or* righteous). The basis of this difference
is not anthropological (what I do or don't do). It is
strictly and solely Christological: to be in Christ
is to be righteous before God."

—Jono Linebaugh[1]

In Christ, I am . . . free.

In Christ, you are . . . free to be holy.

So, my brothers and sisters, you owe the flesh nothing! You do not
need to live according to its ways, *so abandon its oppressive regime.* For
if your life is just about satisfying the impulses of your sinful nature,
then prepare to die. But if you have invited the Spirit to destroy these
selfish desires, you will experience life. If the Spirit of God is leading
you, then *take comfort in knowing* you are His children. (Rom. 8:12–14)

I was raised in competing faith traditions that both focused largely on perfecting oneself through good, old-fashioned strength of will. Ironically, even though each of these faiths points to the other and calls it apostate, both sent me the same message: you'd better be good and believe what we tell you, or God will smite you.

There are a couple of memories that stand out to me as I was growing up torn between these two worlds. One day, when I was about eight, I was talking with an adult about shortcomings. At some point in the conversation I said that no one is perfect. The reply was, "That doesn't mean we shouldn't try to be." I took this to mean that unless I tried to be perfect, I couldn't be saved.

At another junction not far down the road, the war between the two faith traditions came to a head via an unsuspecting woman who was a "counselor" for those who went forward at church during the altar call. I sat with the woman and shared that one side of my family followed a certain religious ideology, and she replied that they were all going to hell and I would, too, if I believed what they were teaching. I remember staring at the blue carpet and crying. I didn't know whom to believe.

I always considered myself a really good Christian kid. I never really rebelled as a youth. I always called home if I was going to be out late, and my mom always knew who I was with. I always went to class and tried to make straight As. I never tried drugs or alcohol, and I didn't have sex. I didn't cuss; I didn't listen to "secular" music. I didn't even see a rated-R movie until I was seventeen. And for all of this, I was pretty proud of myself. But I still didn't feel right or good or happy. All these things did very little to convince me that I was in good standing in God's eyes and did nothing to make me feel that I was worth anything. I lived in constant fear that if I didn't thank God for something, even my ability to see or walk, it would be taken away. I was afraid that if I made one mistake, it would condemn me to the fiery pits for all eternity. God was very important to me, but I didn't yet have any real concept of His love or grace.

My carefully constructed sense of security was founded on my own efforts. I was living the very definition of legalism. If I could go back to teenage me and just sit and talk with her, not only would it mean I had found an actual time machine (and would subsequently become famous), it would perhaps mean I could save myself some of the agony of searching for my identity and worth in myself rather than in Christ. Perhaps I could tell teenage me that no matter what, she was loved, that the Creator of the universe wasn't out to get her. I would try to help that girl see God for who He really is and not the harsh caricature that she had come to believe in.

Even though I didn't sin in the "usual" youthful ways, I was still missing the mark right and left—I was mean to my sisters; I held grudges; I gossiped. I think we've all done a few things we're not proud of. For some of us, our lists of ugly moments might be longer than we care to admit. We've got skeletons in our closets . . . we've got bad habits we can't seem to break . . . we've got a list of things we wish we could do but just can't seem to get right. Many of us are grateful we can't out-sin God's grace, but we simultaneously hate ourselves for having to draw on it as often as we do. Others of us live as though we have forgotten that we're supposed to live differently than our "lost" friends. Maybe some of us get drunk most weekends, have a one-night stand here and there, throw a coworker under the bus when we need to look good, or tell a lie from time to time. But we're all still Christians . . . right?

> Whether we lean toward legalism or we lean toward licentiousness, we've forgotten who we are.

Whether we lean toward legalism or we lean toward licentiousness, we've forgotten who we are. We wallow in guilt, when we've been cleansed of all unrighteousness. Or we waste God's grace, when we've been set free from sin. If we knew who we really are in Christ, our lives would look different than they do. More of us would be living in unwavering obedience

to God because it wouldn't be a burden; we'd simply be acting like who we are.

Saying we're "struggling" with sin implies that sin still has some kind of chance of overtaking us. When we're in Christ, the Spirit empowers us to kill sin rather than simply wrestle with it. "Any temptation you face will be nothing new. But God is faithful, and He will not let you be tempted beyond what you can handle. But He always provides a way of escape so that you will be able to endure *and keep moving forward*. So then, my beloved friends, run from idolatry *in any form*" (1 Cor. 10:13–14). When anything other than God has power over us, we are serving it as a lesser god. Thankfully, being tempted isn't sinful; it's just the result of living in this fallen world. Even Jesus was tempted. But unlike Jesus, we very often succumb to the temptations that come our way.

In my own war with my flesh, it seems each battle is won or lost in a split-second decision.

Are we doomed to sin every time we're tempted? There is always a way of escape if we decide to take it. It is very difficult in those moments when our flesh is warring against the Spirit—difficult to stop and take a step outside of the situation to evaluate what we should do next. So many times it is easier to go to our default, "flesh" reaction and run with it. In my own war with my flesh, it seems each battle is won or lost in a split-second decision. I hate it when I go down the path of sin when all the while the Spirit within is crying out against it. It's almost like an out-of-body experience; I know in my heart that what I'm doing is the total opposite of what I really want to be doing, but there I am, doing it (Paul expressed a similar battle in Romans 7). If I listen to the Spirit and keep looking for the escape route, I can bypass further consequences and take the exit right to God's feet, where I can seek His grace yet again. But in my experience, the longer I wait and the longer I ignore the Spirit's prodding toward that exit, the more difficult it becomes to recognize His voice. Everything starts to get muddy. I start confusing my own wild thoughts with His gentle whispers, and I begin feeling more confused than confident. It is not a fun place to be.

Maybe you know what I'm talking about here. There is probably that "thing" you do that came to mind for you. And I'm going to take a guess and say that you hate that "thing." You hate that fleshly reaction that just seems so natural in so many situations. I want you to know that it is possible to lengthen the time between *temptation* and *reaction* so you can choose a more Spirit-led path. You probably won't choose the Spirit-led path every time in the future, but I pray you know it is possible. In Christ, you are free from both the penalty of sin and the power of sin (Rom. 6:14). Sin doesn't hold you as a slave anymore (Rom. 6:5–7, 22). You absolutely can say no to whatever temptation comes your way. Remember, the power of the living God is what you have access to, and His power crushes any illusion of power that sin has.

We have been freed from the basic law of sin and death because of Jesus' death and resurrection, and thus are adopted as God's children. As God's children, the Holy Spirit resides within us—within our very souls. "Because you are sons, God has sent forth the Spirit of His Son into our hearts, crying, 'Abba! Father!'" (Gal. 4:6 NASB).

Definition of "heart" (*Strong's* [2])

2): the centre and seat of spiritual life

   a) the soul or mind, as it is the fountain and seat of the thoughts, passions, desires, appetites, affections, purposes, endeavours

   b) of the understanding, the faculty and seat of the intelligence

   c) of the will and character

   d) of the soul so far as it is affected and stirred in a bad way or good, or of the soul as the seat of the sensibilities, affections, emotions, desires, appetites, passions

And your heart can cry out to the King of the universe as your Papa.

Having the Creator of the universe, the King of kings, the One True God for our Father . . . that's quite a bit to wrap our minds around, isn't it? It could seem too good to be true or just too intangible. But that doesn't make it any less true. When we're in Christ and Christ is in us, we have this mysterious yet intimately knowable God as our Papa. Many of us have a lot of baggage when it comes to our dads. A lot of us also have a good deal when it comes to our moms. The thing is, God is the perfect Parent. When we're in Christ, He comes alongside us and wants to fill every familial void ever left within us. No longer are we alone or left without the love we so deeply crave. No longer are we left to fend for ourselves. No longer are we abandoned or ignored or peripheral or beat down. We are loved more deeply than we can ever fathom.

> If the Spirit of God is leading you, then *take comfort in knowing* you are His children. You see, you have not received a spirit that returns you to slavery, so you have nothing to fear. The Spirit you have received adopts you *and welcomes you* into God's own family. That's why we call out to Him, "Abba! Father!" *as we would address a loving daddy. Through that prayer,* God's Spirit confirms in our spirits that we are His children. If we are God's children, that means we are His heirs along with the Anointed, set to inherit everything that is His. If we share His sufferings, *we know that* we will ultimately share in His glory. (Rom. 8:14–17)

Having the King of the universe for our Dad has all kinds of implications. Not only are we indescribably loved; we're set free to live as though we know it is true. When we live as if we know we're unconditionally loved, something about us changes. When we respect someone, we tend to want to please that person. In Christ, we don't want to "be good" to stay out of trouble; we want to lead lives permeated by the love we know. And part of being in Christ is allowing God to rearrange us and shape us more into His likeness.

Indeed, you seem to have forgotten the proverb directed to you as children:

> My child, do not ignore the instruction that
> comes from the Lord,
> or lose heart when He steps in to correct you;
> For the Lord disciplines those He loves,
> and He corrects each one He takes as His
> own

Endure hardship as God's discipline and rejoice that He is treating you as His children, for what child doesn't experience discipline from a parent? But if you are not experiencing the correction that all true children receive, then it may be that you are not His children after all. Remember, when our human parents disciplined us, we respected them. *If that was true*, shouldn't we respect and live under the correction of the Father of all spirits even more? Our parents corrected us for a time as seemed good to them, but God only corrects us to our good so that we may share in His holiness. (Heb. 12:5–10)

For the moment all discipline seems painful rather than pleasant, but later it yields the peaceful fruit of righteousness to those who have been trained by it. (Heb. 12:11 ESV)

These verses describe a really valuable aspect of God as our Parent. I don't know about you, but I am not so sure I respected my parents when they disciplined me! Even so, the Bible clearly teaches I should not only respect God, but rejoice when He disciplines me. How can I wrap my mind around that? The word translated *discipline* in these verses is the Greek word *paideia*. Check out the *Strong's* definition:[3]

1. the whole training and education of children (which relates to the cultivation of mind and morals, and employs for this purpose now commands and admonitions, now reproof and punishment) . . . It also includes the training and care of the body . . .

2. "whatever in adults also cultivates the soul, esp. by correcting mistakes and curbing passions" . . .

a. instruction which aims at the increase of virtue

b. . . . chastisement, chastening, (of the evils with which God visits men for their amendment)[3]

As we've established, in Christ the punishment for sin has been taken care of; Jesus absorbed God's wrath on our behalf. Discipline, however, is something we must continue to pursue as we follow Jesus because it means we're being trained, educated, and cultivated. That takes on a much different tone than punishment, doesn't it? Now, discipline can include painful experiences. Who among us hasn't had to live with the consequences of her actions and hated it? "Later, though it yields the peaceful fruit called righteousness" (Heb. 12:11) and is "to our good so that we may share in [Christ's] holiness" (v. 10). In addition to allowing us to bear the natural consequences of our decisions, God often uses things outside of our control to shape us more into His likeness. For me, I know I'm being refined when nothing seems to be going my way—everything in my life just feels like it is going wrong, even though I've been faithful in seeking God the best I know how. Often during those times God is taking me into a deeper level of trust in Him, and quite honestly, usually those aren't fun times. But later when I look back, I see how gracious God was in cutting away parts of myself that didn't reflect His character. If we're experiencing a time of correction or refinement, it means God really, truly cares about us and we're really, truly in Christ. That is cause to rejoice.

> *I see how gracious God was in cutting away parts of myself that didn't reflect His character.*

★　★　★

One of the words used throughout the New Testament for believers or followers of Christ is *saints*. I don't know about you, but this brings a few different images to mind for me. I grew up in New Mexico in a culture that was heavily Catholic. For a long time when I thought of saints I thought of

the beautiful necklaces many of my Catholic friends wore, small emblems of highly esteemed people in their faith. Many of my friends had been named for saints. So in my mind, saints were heroes: extremely good people who managed to lead extraordinarily holy lives, some even going so far as to die as martyrs. And I would never have dreamed of including myself among these people. It was ludicrous. Who would put themselves on the same level as the apostles, Saint Patrick, Augustine, Francis of Assisi, or Joan of Arc?

Paul, Luke, Jude, John, and the writer of Hebrews all used the term *saint* in their writings to refer in general to followers of Jesus—those who are in Christ. Their letters predate the process of canonizing saints, so I think we should take a look at what they had in mind when they used this word. The Greek word translated *saints* is *hagios*, the same word that translates as *holy* in other places in the New Testament. It designates that something or someone has been separated and set apart for a particular purpose and should be treated as sacred and holy. This holiness isn't something that is attained—it simply is. So, when we are in Christ, we are saints, not because we do things that make us saintly, but because God has said we are. And He implores us, as saints, to act accordingly—to live as if we know who we really are.

Read the definition of *hagios* in a Bible dictionary or concordance, such as *Strong's* or *Vine's*. You can find these and other language tools at www.blueletterbible.com or www.mystudybible.com. How does the definition of this word change the way you view Christians in general, and yourself specifically?

What would it look like if we started defining ourselves like this? What if we started defining ourselves based on who we are in Christ? Does someone come to mind for you when you think of that—someone who lives as though she really truly believes that she is worthy of the calling she has in Christ? She lives with the constant humility of knowing she can fall into sin just as easily as anyone else, but that isn't her focus. She isn't happy to just live a docile life, knowing she's destined for heaven and happy to say a little prayer of thanks to God now and then. She is IN CHRIST, and she lives like it. She takes chances loving people because she knows it is what Jesus would do. She looks evil in the face and doesn't shy away because she knows that when she is in Christ, He fights the battle alongside her. She listens to the Holy Spirit's voice above all the rest and lets everybody else's opinions bounce off of her.

I want to be like that.

Paul

There are volumes written about Paul. He was a fascinating person, for sure. As if receiving a miraculous call from Jesus and writing a great deal of the New Testament weren't enough, he was "circumcised on the eighth day, of the people of Israel, of the tribe of Benjamin, a Hebrew of Hebrews; as to the law, a Pharisee; as to zeal, a persecutor of the church; as to righteousness under the law, blameless" (Phil. 3:5–6 ESV). But wait . . . what was that about being a persecutor of the church?

We often gloss over the fact that Paul had a very sordid past. You may recall that throughout his early days, Paul was known as Saul. As Saul, he oversaw the murder of people who followed Jesus. In fact, while Stephen was becoming the first Christian martyr, Saul watched the angry mob's coats (Acts 7:58). He barged into people's homes and dragged them off to prison, men and women alike (Acts 8:3). Saul sought the highest authorities to help him weed out Christians wherever he could find them (Acts

9:1–2). And then he met Jesus. Nothing was ever the same for him ever again.

"And when he had come to Jerusalem, he attempted to join the disciples. And they were all afraid of him, for they did not believe that he was a disciple" (Acts 9:26 ESV). Yeah, I think I would be scared too. As a dual citizen of both Palestine and Rome, Paul could use both his Hebrew name, Saul, and his Latin name, Paul. It probably made more sense for him to go by his Latin name once he began to focus on his mission to the Gentiles. But I do wonder if Paul was relieved to be able to go by another name after all he'd done as Saul.

If anyone understood the power of God's grace, it was Paul. Though he was still human and still fought against sin, he understood the cleansing work of Jesus in his life. The Holy Spirit has worked dramatic moments of sanctification in many of our lives, while for others of us the process of refinement has been more drawn out. No matter what, being purified isn't really that fun, and it is often painful. Sometimes it feels as if we go three steps forward and two steps back. In a moment we will read Paul's description of that ongoing battle with the flesh. But as we allow the Spirit to shape us and remove the parts of us that aren't like Jesus, we experience more and more victory over temptation. The more practice we have in following the Spirit's lead instead of our own, the more we will realize who we are as God's chosen, holy people: His saints.

As we allow the Spirit to shape us and remove the parts of us that aren't like Jesus, we experience more and more victory over temptation.

Step into the Story

Before you dive into Romans 7, read Romans 6 for context.

Romans 7

¹ My brothers and sisters who are well versed in the law, don't you realize that a person is subject to the law only as long as he is alive? ² So, for example, a wife is obligated by the law to her husband until his death; if the husband dies, she is freed from the parts of the law that relate to her marriage. ³ If she is sleeping with another man while her husband is alive, she is rightly labeled an adulteress. But if her husband dies, she is free from the law and can marry another man. In such a case, she is not an adulteress.

---

vv. 4–6

STANDOUT MOMENTS:

We aren't "married" to the law; we're "married" to Christ. As the bride of Christ, we belong to Him and are free to live in a totally different way than we did before. We're Spirit-empowered now, instead of flesh-empowered.

---

⁴ My brothers and sisters, in the same way, you have died when it comes to the law because of *your connection with* the body of the Anointed One. His death—*and your death with Him*—frees you to belong to the One who was raised from the dead so we can bear fruit for God. ⁵ As we were living in the flesh, the law *could not solve the problem of sin; it* only awakened our lust for more and cultivated the fruit of death in our bodily members. ⁶ But now that we have died to those chains that imprisoned us, we have been released from the law to serve in a new Spirit-empowered life, not the old written code.

⁷ So what is the story? Is the law itself sin? Absolutely not! *It is the exact opposite.* I would never have known what sin is if it were not for the law. *For example,* I would not have known that desiring something that

belongs to my neighbor is sin if the law had not said, "You are not to covet." ⁸ Sin took advantage of the commandment to create a constant stream of greed and desire within me; *I began to want everything.* You see, apart from the law, sin lies dormant. ⁹ There was a time when I was living without the law, but the commandment came *and changed everything*: sin came to life, and I died. ¹⁰ This commandment was supposed to bring life; but in my experience, it brought death. ¹¹ Sin took advantage of the commandment, tricked me, and exploited it in order to kill me. ¹² So *hear me out:* the law is holy; and its commandments are holy, right, and good.

¹³ So did the good *law* bring about my death? Absolutely not! It was sin that killed me, *not the law.* It's the nature of sin to produce death through what is good and exploit the commandments to multiply sin's vile effects. ¹⁴ This is what we know: the law comes from the spiritual realm. *My problem is that* I am of the fallen human realm, owned by sin, *which tries to keep me in its service.*

¹⁵ *Listen,* I can't explain my actions. Here's why: I am not able to do the things I want; and at the same time, I do the things I despise. ¹⁶ If I am doing the things I have already decided not to do, I am agreeing with the law regarding what is good. ¹⁷ But now I am no longer the one acting—*I've lost control*—sin has taken up residence in me *and is wreaking havoc.* ¹⁸ I know that in me, that is, in my fallen human nature, there is nothing good. I can will myself to do something good, but that does not help me carry it out. ¹⁹ I can determine that I am going to do good, but I don't do it; instead, I end up living out the evil that I decided not to do. ²⁰ If I end up doing the exact thing I pledged not to do, I am no longer doing it because sin has taken up residence in me.

²¹ Here's an *important* principle I've discovered: regardless of my desire to do the right thing, *it is clear that* evil is never far away. ²² For deep down I am in happy agreement with God's law; ²³ but the rest of

vv. 13–14

BIG PICTURE:

It is the nature of Satan to seek what is good and attempt to ruin it. Our sinful nature takes good things and twists them to our own detriment. When God gave the law, He wasn't setting people up for failure but was instead showing us our need for a Savior.

me does not concur. I see a very different principle at work in my bodily members, and it is at war with my mind; I have become a prisoner in this war to the rule of sin in my body. ²⁴ I am absolutely miserable! Is there anyone who can free me from this body where *sin and* death reign *so supremely?* ²⁵ I am thankful to God *for the freedom that comes* through our Lord Jesus, the Anointed One! So on the one hand, I devotedly serve God's law with my mind; but on the other hand, with my flesh, I serve the principle of sin.

 **PRAYER**

 **BIG PICTURE**

 **CONTEXT**

 **ORIGINAL AUDIENCE**

 **STAND OUT MOMENTS**

v. 25

CONTEXT:

Be sure to read Romans 8:1 to see where Paul goes next. Thank God for grace!

Come Together

❖ What part of your flesh needs to be put under the control of the Holy Spirit?

❖ When was a time that you were able to resist temptation? How did it feel to say no and follow the Spirit instead?

❖ Have you gone through a specific time of discipline from the Lord? What was that like? What was your relationship with God like afterward?

❖ Share a "Standout Moment" from this chapter and what you will do as a result.

Sin and the child of God are incompatible. They may occasionally meet; they cannot live together in harmony.

—John Stott[4]

Notes

CHAPTER SIX

Peacemaker

As I have said, the first thing is to be honest with
yourself. You can never have an impact on society if
you have not changed yourself . . . Great peacemakers
are all people of integrity, of honesty, but humility.

—attributed to Nelson Mandela

In Christ, I am . . . a victorious peacemaker.

In Christ, you are . . . a victorious peacemaker.

So what should we say about all of this? If God is on our side, *then
tell me*: whom should we fear? If He did not spare His own Son, but
handed Him over on our account, then *don't you think that* He will
graciously give us all things with Him? Can anyone be so bold as to
level a charge against God's chosen? *Especially since* God's *"not guilty"*
verdict is already declared. Who has the authority to condemn? Jesus
the Anointed who died, but *more importantly, conquered death when He*
was raised to sit at the right hand of God where He pleads on our
behalf. So who can separate us? What can come between us and the
love of God's Anointed? Can troubles, hardships, persecution, hunger, poverty, danger, or even death? *The answer is, absolutely nothing.* As
the psalm says,

On Your behalf, our lives are endangered constantly;
we are like sheep awaiting slaughter.

But no matter what comes, we will always taste victory through
Him who loved us. (Rom. 8:31–37)

Do you believe Satan exists? What role do you think he plays in
your life? How about demons? Do you wake up each morning and think,
Hey, I'm in a spiritual war? It may sound crazy, but you are indeed in one,
whether or not you realize it. And Satan has a plan for your life.

The Bible uses terms like "adversary" and "accuser" to describe Satan,
and paints a picture of lying, malicious evil incarnate. He isn't just some
guy in a red suit with pointy horns and a pitchfork. He is real. And while
we need not fear him, we must take him seriously. What is Satan's ultimate goal for us as believers? He wants to influence us as much as he can
in order to hurt God. There is no good intent in him whatsoever. How
much access does he have to us? If we are in Christ, Satan can't touch our
souls, he can't control us, he can't read our minds, and he can't level anything at us that God hasn't preapproved. While God doesn't cause evil, at
times He chooses to allow it, not only for our own good but also for His
glory. For His children, God uses Satan's schemes against him and turns
his attacks into blessings.

When it comes to warring against Satan, time and again we are told
to fight, stand our ground, and be brave. We're also reminded that it is
God who fights our battles for us. Now, what about our interaction with
the rest of the world? Paul wrote that "we do not wrestle against flesh and
blood, but against the rulers, against the authorities, against the cosmic
powers over this present darkness, against the spiritual forces of evil in the
heavenly places" (Eph. 6:12 ESV). If Satan is the real enemy, how should
we view other people—especially the people our society or culture calls
our enemies?

"Blessed are the peacemakers—they will be called children of God."
(Matt. 5:9)

These are Jesus' words. The word He used for "peacemakers" is the Greek word *eirenepoios*. And this is the only time we ever see it in the New Testament. So should we make a big deal out of it, or pass it off as not that important of a concept? I think that since the idea of being at peace with those around us is a theme that runs throughout the New Testament, we should pay attention to what Jesus said here. Peacemakers will be called children of God. Ultimately that is who we are in Christ, isn't it? Children of God? So it stands to reason that we should thus be viewed as seekers of peace.

Unfortunately I think this is not quite the reputation we Christians have in the United States. We're known more for fighting among ourselves, hating sinners, and boycotting. I don't know about you, but that's not really what I signed up for. I would much rather be known as someone who loved people to the very end, whether they were my brothers and sisters in Christ or the pariahs of society. I would rather be known as someone who could help peacefully moderate arguments, and not as someone on the hunt for starting them.

What else did Jesus have to say about seeking peace?

> "You have been taught to love your neighbor and hate your enemy. But I tell you this: love your enemies. Pray for those who torment you and persecute you—in so doing, you become children of your Father in heaven. *He, after all, loves each of us—good and evil, kind and cruel.* He causes the sun to rise *and shine* on evil and good alike. He causes the rain *to water the fields* of the righteous and *the fields* of the sinner. It is easy to love those who love you—even a tax collector can love those who love him. And it is easy to greet your friends—even outsiders do that! *But you are called to something higher:* 'Be perfect, as your Father in heaven is perfect.'" (Matt. 5:43–48)

Jesus indicated that loving our enemies is involved in "perfection"; that is, completion and maturity. And again He indicated peace-seeking is a hallmark of God's children. Throughout Matthew 5, Jesus taught that fulfillment of the law has to do with the heart and not just outward actions,

taking the high road rather than seeking revenge, seeking the good of those who hate us, and not simply paying God lip service. A "perfect" person in Christ is not one who never makes mistakes, but one who strives to be Christlike in any given situation. When we are secure in who we are and whose we are, we are more likely to draw from the Holy Spirit for our responses and reactions.

> A "perfect" person in Christ is not one who never makes mistakes, but one who strives to be Christlike in any given situation.

One Saturday afternoon my husband and I were having a late lunch with our son at a twenty-four-hour restaurant. After we ordered our meals, I noticed the person sitting at the table next to us. We'll call her Shari. She was probably in her fifties, with shoulder-length, tangled gray hair. She wore a bright purple-and-blue muumuu over a pair of hospital scrubs, worn sandals, and several layers of plastic beads. Draped over the chair across from Shari were her belongings—a bright-pink-and-turquoise coat, a handbag made out of bright-pink sequins, a neon-orange hat, and a shopping bag full of various articles, including personal care items and canned food. It was clear that the other restaurant patrons were avoiding her. As she interacted with the server, we noticed her sweet disposition and a few other things—she didn't seem to know what year it was, and though she paid with cash, she asked to sign the sales receipt with her lipstick. At one point I noticed that she was grinding her teeth so hard that it was audible.

Smiling, Shari noticed our son and asked me how old he was. At that moment I had a choice: I could answer the question politely and move my seat to where I would be less accessible for conversation, or I could engage with Shari and give her my full attention. I went with the latter. Throughout our disjointed conversation I learned that she had a son of her own, but the way she talked about him I wondered if perhaps he had died as a small child. When she asked my son's name, she took it as an opportunity to share every fact she knew about the name David. I noticed the people around us began to relax as Shari and I talked. When it was time to part ways, Shari had tears in her eyes as she thanked me for talking with her, and I told her that I was glad to have met her.

Most of us wouldn't have called Shari an "enemy," but we might have treated her as a nuisance or threat and tried to avoid her as we would an enemy. Isn't it interesting how, once we move past initial fears about people who are vastly different from us, we come to see the humanity in them? There may be types of people whom you strongly dislike or even despise—the homeless, the homosexual, the religious fanatic, the wealthy, the liberal, the conservative . . . Could it be because you don't have any friends who fall into those particular categories? It's a challenge we all need to take up—the challenge to befriend those who make us uncomfortable and extend Christ's love to them.

"When Jesus talks about loving the enemy, he is talking about working to create something new. Creating a new identity through unity. When you have this new identity, the concept of 'the other' is completely eliminated . . . Jesus could have said, 'Resolve your problems with your enemy.' But he said, 'Love your enemy.' . . . Their sorrows become your sorrows, their history becomes your history, and their future becomes your future."[1] What is your reaction to this concept?

While He preached love for enemies, Jesus certainly didn't shy away from His adversaries. He took the religious leaders of His day head-on when they set their traps for Him. He also said He didn't come to bring peace. How do we reconcile this with His teachings and life of nonviolence?

Do not imagine that I have come to bring peace to the earth. I did not come to bring peace, but a sword. I have come to turn men against their fathers, daughters against their mothers, and daughters-in-law against their mothers-in-law. You will find you have enemies even in your own household. If you love your father or mother more than you love Me, then you are not worthy of Me. If you love your son or daughter more than you love Me, then you are not worthy of Me. If you refuse to take up your cross and follow Me *on the narrow road*, then you are not worthy of Me. To find your life, you must lose your life—and whoever loses his life for My sake will find it. (Matt. 10:34–39)

Jesus was communicating to the disciples about what they were going to experience as they went out into the world in His name. He warned them about the people who would oppose them and about the fact that they would experience persecution because of Him. He even told them to be careful:

"Listen: I am sending you out to be sheep among wolves. You must be as shrewd as serpents and as innocent as doves. You must be careful. You must be discerning. You must be on your guard. There will be men who try to hand you over to their town councils and have you flogged in their synagogues. Because of Me, naysayers and doubters will try to make an example out of you by trying you before rulers and kings. When this happens—*when you are arrested, dragged to court*—don't worry about what to say or how to say it. The words you should speak will be given to you. For at that moment, it will not be you speaking; it will be the Spirit of your Father speaking through you." (Matt. 10:16–20)

So Jesus wasn't condoning a generally divisive, argumentative, warlike attitude. He was basically telling the disciples to weigh the cost of following Him. He told them that if they weren't willing to abandon everything for Him, they should just stay home.

Conflict is going to be a reality for us as those who are in Christ. While we are not to provoke (1 Cor. 13:4–7), if we're faithfully following Him, eventually we are going to rub people the wrong way. There really isn't any way around that. But any discomfort that our presence might bring people should be because we are drenched in the Holy Spirit and exude God's love. We will meet people who strongly react to the Spirit within us because it doesn't make sense to them (John 7:7; 17:14). We will be hated because we love Jesus—we know that much is true (Mark 13:13; Luke 21:17; 1 John 3:13). The world will know we follow Him because of our love for one another in Christ (John 13:35). They will know we follow Him because our lives will show it. And even if they hate us for it, we are to love them in return.

What did Paul have to say about peacemaking? His words echo Jesus' words:

> If people mistreat or malign you, bless them. Always speak blessings, not curses. If some have cause to celebrate, join in the celebration. And if others are weeping, join in that as well. Work toward unity, and live in harmony with one another. Avoid thinking you are better than others or wiser than the rest; instead, embrace common people *and ordinary tasks.* Do not retaliate with evil, regardless of the evil brought against you. Try to do what is good *and right and honorable* as agreed upon by all people. If it is within your power, make peace with all people. (Rom. 12:14–18)

And again Paul wrote:

> He died for us so that we will all live, not for ourselves, but for Him who died and rose from the dead. *Because of all that God has done,* we now have a new perspective. We used to show regard for people based on worldly standards and interests. No longer. We used to think of the Anointed the same way. No longer. Therefore, if anyone is united with the Anointed One, that person is a new creation. The old life is gone—and see—a new life has begun! All of this is *a gift* from *our Creator* God, who has *pursued us and* brought us into a restored *and healthy* relationship with Him through the Anointed. And He has given us *the same mission,* the ministry of reconciliation, *to bring others back to Him. It is central to our good news* that God was in the Anointed making things right

between Himself and the world. This means He does not hold their sins against them. But it also means He charges us to proclaim the message that heals and restores our broken relationships *with God and each other*.

So we are now representatives of the Anointed One, *the Liberating King;* God has given us a charge to carry through our lives—urging all people on behalf of the Anointed to become reconciled to *the Creator* God. He orchestrated this: the *Anointed* One, who had never experienced sin, became sin for us so that in Him we might embody the very righteousness of God. (2 Cor. 5:15–21)

These passages, like so many others, reiterate that we must be peacemakers, ambassadors on God's behalf, who plead with people to reach out to Christ to rescue them. Remember the great story that God is weaving, the one that culminates in His ultimate glory? It is all about reconciliation and setting things right. It is all about redemption. It is all about making people, relationships, and this very world brand-new. God is about creating. Violence in any of its forms, whether it be physical, sexual, emotional, spiritual, or verbal, is the opposite of creating. As peacemakers, we must vehemently oppose violence because it tears apart God's heart for us as His most treasured creation. As peacemakers we must be about the business of bringing people together with one another and, through the good news of Jesus Christ the Anointed, point the way back to God.

What is at stake when we fail to seek peace and reconciliation in the world around us? James gave a description of what our lives could look like when we live outside God's leading toward peace:

> My brothers and sisters, does a fig tree produce olives? Is there a grapevine capable of growing figs? Can salt water give way to freshwater?
>
> Who in your community is understanding and wise? Let his example, which is marked by wisdom and gentleness, blaze a trail for others. If your heart is one that bleeds dark streams of jealousy and selfishness, do not be so proud that you ignore your depraved state. The wisdom of this world should never be mistaken for heavenly wisdom; it originates below in the earthly realms, with the demons. Any place where you find jealousy and selfish ambition, you will discover chaos and evil

thriving under its rule. Heavenly wisdom centers on purity, peace, gentleness, deference, mercy, and other good fruits untainted by hypocrisy. The seed that flowers into righteousness will always be planted in peace by those who embrace peace.

Where do you think your fighting and *endless* conflict come from? Don't you think that they originate in the *constant pursuit of* gratification that rages inside each of you *like an uncontrolled militia*? You crave something that you do not possess, so you murder to get it. You desire the things you cannot earn, so you *sue others and* fight for what you want. You do not have because you have chosen not to ask. And when you do ask, you still do not get what you want because your motives are all wrong—because you continually focus on self-indulgence. You are adulterers. Don't you know that making friends with this corrupt world order is open aggression toward God? So anyone who aligns with this bogus world system is declaring war against the one true God. Do you think it is empty rhetoric when the Scriptures say, "The spirit that lives in us is addicted to envy and jealousy"? *You may think that the situation is hopeless,* but God gives us more grace *when we turn away from our own interests.* That's why Scripture says,

> God opposes the proud,
> but He pours out grace on the humble.

So submit yourselves to the one true God and fight against the devil *and his schemes.* If you do, he will run away *in failure.* (James 3:12–4:7)

James was speaking mainly to us about how we treat others who are in Christ. The description he gave there in chapters 3 and 4 is pretty scary to me. If we view one another as being in Christ along with us, the way we treat each other should be a beacon of hope and belonging, not only for those within the family of God, but also to those outside of it. "The seed that flowers into righteousness will always be planted in peace by those who embrace peace" (James 3:18). But many of us, among fellow believers, have experienced some of the jealousy (3:16), selfish ambition (3:16), fighting (4:1), endless conflict (4:1), and constant pursuit of selfish gratification (4:3) that James described as chaotic evil (3:16) and the devil's schemes

(4:7). Some of our churches war among themselves over all sorts of things, and not only does it create an environment of hostility within those church bodies, the warlike attitude spills over into the surrounding communities. These churches and their members become known for what they hate, not whom they love. People who are living in this kind of selfishness are "align[ed] with this bogus world system [and] declaring war against the one true God" (James 4:4). It is easy for me to point the finger at others who are guilty of this, but I have to be willing to look at myself too. Am I more willing to fight for my own comfort, opinions, and preferences than I am for those of others? Friends, we have to get this right. We have to get over our addiction to self-gratification and self-prioritization. God is ready to pour out grace on us if we submit ourselves to Him in humility and recognize that we do not need to fight against the Body of Christ, but against Satan (James 4:6–7). Imagine what God could do through us if we were united together in peace rather than wasting time making a mockery of ourselves (and Him) with our bickering. The devil would run away in failure (James 4:7)!

> We have to get over our addiction to self-gratification and self-prioritization.

So, what does making peace look like? Do we all just become doormats? Do we stand idly by if a fellow believer is living in self-destruct mode just to "keep the peace"? Making peace does not mean we turn a blind eye to injustice, sin, or evil. Being a peacemaking part of the Body of Christ involves hard work and often even struggle. We have to love each other enough to deal with the messier parts of our lives in order to bring repentance and healing (Prov. 27:5; Luke 17:3; Gal. 6:2; James 5:16).

We will always live with the tension of loving those who aren't in Christ, yet resisting the temptation to align ourselves with this "corrupt world order" (James 4:4). This is why we are both warriors and peacemakers. We are at war with the world and its master, but we should be at peace with each other. We have to know who our real enemy is. Our enemies aren't people, but Satan and his minions, who seek to influence people. If that's the case, we must be very careful how we approach and interact with those who aren't in Christ; as Paul wrote in Colossians 4:5–6, "Be wise when you engage with those outside *the faith community*; make the most of every moment *and every encounter.* When you speak the word, speak it gracefully (as if seasoned with salt), so you will know how to respond to everyone rightly." If we're a part of a local church body that is healthy, we will hopefully have lots of examples of this kind of communication all around us. We will have friends in that church who ooze grace, know the culture of the community, have broken free of ethnocentrism (the attitude that one's own group is superior), and can interact with anyone from any background. These are the folks who are deeply rooted in Christ and make no bones about it, but who love God and others so much they are actually pleasant to be around. That's the kind of person I want to spend my time with. It's the kind of person I want to be.

Barnabas

His name was Joseph. We know him as Barnabas, which means "son of encouragement." The apostles had given him this nickname when the church had just begun. Barnabas sold a piece of property he owned and donated the proceeds toward the work of caring for his brothers and sisters. He must have just had one of those personalities that endeared people to him. We know for sure that he was a brave man of God[3] because he was the only one not afraid of Saul.

Recall that Saul/Paul encountered Jesus on the road to Damascus and had a dramatic conversion. After spending some time in Damascus preaching the very gospel he had so violently opposed, he got wind that there were some people there plotting to kill him. They didn't like this new Saul. So some of Saul's new friends helped him escape one night, and Saul headed for what could have seemed like the most logical place to go—Jerusalem, the hub of those following the Way.

I wonder if Saul went to Jerusalem as a last resort or with hope of being accepted? Whatever the situation, he tried to join with the disciples there "but they were all afraid of him, not believing that he was a disciple" (Acts 9:26 NASB). Now, based on what we know, can we really blame them? Perhaps they thought he was faking belief in order to get more information and kill them all. I imagine many of us in the same situation would be at least standoffish. "But Barnabas took hold of him and brought him to the apostles and described to them how he had seen the Lord on the road, and that He had talked to him, and how at Damascus he had spoken out boldly in the name of Jesus" (Acts 9:27 NASB). Can you see the scene? I wonder if Barnabas even physically (but compassionately) dragged a reluctant Saul to the apostles. Barnabas saw the truth: Saul had indeed encountered the living God and followed Him wholeheartedly. Barnabas advocated for Saul and believed him. He knew that Saul was risking his life for the gospel, and he told the other disciples so.

Can you imagine where the world would be if Barnabas hadn't come alongside Paul and stood up for him? Obviously God still would have accomplished all He intended to through Paul, but I can't imagine what Paul's life would have been like if he had never been vetted by the apostles and other disciples in Jerusalem. Thankfully, Barnabas listened to the Spirit's leading and took a leap of faith for Paul.

We never know what purposes and plans God has for a person. The people we view as scary, different, difficult, hardened, or even violent may be the very people God has marked for His mission. The most vocal atheist you know might just be the next great Christian evangelist. It is important that we never give up hope and that we never become so cynical that we miss out on the possibilities of God's powerful love. We can be both bold and compassionate in our witness.

Step into the Story

Romans 13

It is important that all of us submit to the authorities who have charge over us because God establishes all authority *in heaven and on the earth*. ² Therefore, a person who rebels against authority rebels against the order He established, and people like that can expect to face certain judgment. ³ You see, if you do the right thing, you have nothing to be worried about from the rulers; but if you do what you know is wrong, the rulers will make sure you pay a price. Would you not rather live with a clear conscience than always have to be looking over your shoulder? Then keep doing what you know to be good and right, and they will publicly honor you.

⁴ *Look at it this way*: The ruler is a servant of God called to serve and benefit you. But he is also a servant of God executing wrath upon those who practice evil. If you do what is wrong, then you'd better be afraid because he wields the power of the sword and doesn't make empty threats.

⁵ So submission is not optional; it's required. But don't just submit for the sake of avoiding punishment; submit *and abide by the laws* because your conscience leads you to do the right thing. ⁶ Pay your taxes for the same reason because the authorities are servants of God, giving their full attention to take care of these things. ⁷ Pay all of them

vv. 1, 5

STANDOUT MOMENTS:

We are to be respectful of those in office whether we voted for them or not. We may not agree with them and may even oppose the decisions they make, but we must do so respectfully. Remember, our war is not with earthly authorities.

vv. 5–6

BIG PICTURE:

Abiding by the laws of the land is important for us to do. Check out Matthew 22:15–22. There may be laws that are passed that violate what the Bible teaches, and in those cases we must of course submit to God instead.

what you owe. If you owe taxes, then pay. If you owe fees, then pay. In the same way, give honor and respect to those who deserve it.

vv. 8–10

PRAYER:

Father, thank You for making it is so simple to "achieve everything the law requires," but thank You also for not expecting us to do it on our own power. Help me to love You and love others more fully.

⁸ Don't owe anyone anything, with the exception of love to one another—*that is a debt which never ends*—because the person who loves others has fulfilled the law. ⁹ The commands *given to you in the Scriptures*—do not commit adultery, do not murder, do not take what is not yours, do not covet—and any other command *you have heard* are summarized in God's instruction: "Love your neighbor as yourself." ¹⁰ Does love hurt anyone? Absolutely not. In fact, love achieves everything the law requires.

¹¹ And *now consider* this. You know well the times *you are living in*. It is time for you to wake up *and see what is right before your eyes*: for salvation is nearer to us now than when we first believed. ¹² The darkness of night is dissolving as dawn's light draws near, so walk out on your old dark life and put on the armor of light. ¹³ May we all act as good and respectable people, living today the same way as we will in the day *of His coming*. Do not fall into patterns of dark living: wild partying, drunkenness, sexual depravity, decadent gratification, quarreling, and jealousy. ¹⁴ Instead, wrap yourselves in the Lord Jesus, God's Anointed, and do not fuel your sinful imagination by indulging *your self-seeking desire* for the pleasures of the flesh.

vv. 11–14

ORIGINAL AUDIENCE:

Living in Rome, it would have been considered normal to be a part of the types of things listed in verse 13, much as it is now. Paul encouraged believers to live counterculturally and be wrapped up with Jesus instead of "the good life."

 **PRAYER**

 **BIG PICTURE**

 **CONTEXT**

 **ORIGINAL AUDIENCE**

 **STAND OUT MOMENTS**

Come Together

❖ What does spiritual warfare look like? When was a time you experienced it yourself? (Take care to make this a conversation of understanding and unity rather than divisiveness, especially if you and your friends come from different faith backgrounds.)

❖ What is Satan's ultimate goal for us as believers?

❖ Whom would you consider an "enemy," and how might God be calling you to love that person or people group? What is a first step you can take toward this goal?

❖ Share a "Standout Moment" from this chapter and what you will do as a result.

> *S*trive for peace with everyone, and for the holiness without which no one will see the Lord.
>
> **—Hebrews 12:14 ESV**

Notes

CHAPTER SEVEN

From childhood's hour I have not been

As others were; I have not seen

As others saw; I could not bring

My passions from a common spring.

From the same source I have not taken

My sorrow; I could not awaken

My heart to joy at the same tone;

And all I loved, I loved alone.

—Edgar Allan Poe[1]

In Christ, I am . . . a part of a family.

In Christ, you are . . . a part of a family.

You see, you have not received a spirit that returns you to slavery, so you have nothing to fear. The Spirit you have received adopts you

and welcomes you into God's own family. That's why we call out to Him, "Abba! Father!" *as we would address a loving daddy. Through that prayer,* God's Spirit confirms in our spirits that we are His children. If we are God's children, that means we are His heirs along with the Anointed, set to inherit everything that is His. If we share His sufferings, *we know that* we will ultimately share in His glory. (Rom. 8:15–17)

To this day very little gets me more scared and anxious than a thunderstorm. When I was really young, I would go into my parents' bedroom and crawl into bed with them and feel safe, as if everything was going to be just fine and nothing would touch us. I was safe and secure there.

Then, when I was six, my parents divorced. There was a period of time when my two younger sisters and I stayed with some friends of the family—I think it was just a night or two, but to me it felt like at least a month. I vividly recall there being a storm one night. I couldn't run to my parents.

> *I'm still learning to allow myself to be a needy part of the Body of Christ now and then.*

I didn't know if I would ever be with them again. I got up from where I'd been sleeping and tiptoed in the dark toward my friend's parents' room. I remember standing in their doorway as lightning flashed outside the window and rain poured down, casting shadows upon them as they slept in their bed. For an instant I thought about waking them up to tell them how scared I was. But then I realized I had no right to do so. They weren't my parents. In that instant, my little heart hardened and I knew I had to just make it through that scary night on my own. There was no one there to make me feel safe. I can pinpoint that moment in my life when I came to believe that I was totally alone, on my own, and had to take care of myself.

I carried that hardened, scared, self-reliant mentality through the rest of my life. The lie that I was totally on my own was so ingrained in me that I didn't even really realize it was there until I was dating my now husband. One evening as we were talking, I realized that he was the first

person with which I had ever felt totally and completely safe. I trust very few people. To this day
trust is a value on which I have to work to embrace.
While I am very open about my past, there are
probably only two or three people in the world I
would ever share my current struggles or my hopes
and dreams for the future. On the one hand, that
is appropriate—we don't need the whole world in
our business. But on the other hand, it makes me a bit lonely at times.
I'm still learning to allow myself to be a needy part of the Body of Christ
now and then.

I often feel like a wanderer without a tribe.

Although I have always had a close bond with both of my sisters, I
never really felt that I fit in anywhere growing up. When I was a pre-teen
I always found adults more interesting for conversation than people my
own age. I was the floater when it came to cliques in high school. I had
good friends in many circles—one friend was on track to be valedictorian,
another was a star on the football team, and another was gay. I had junkie
friends, smart friends, theater friends, and I mostly spent time with my
chorus friends. I had a couple of Christian friends, but could count them
on one hand. I loved (and still love) having people from such a wide array
of backgrounds and interests in my life. But I didn't feel I fit 100 percent
into any one group. College was the same way. Especially since I usually
was in some kind of leadership role, it was very difficult for me to ever
really immerse myself in one group or another. Even now, I often feel like
a wanderer without a tribe. One reason for this is that a fear of abandon-
ment still tends to run deep in me, and with the transient nature of our
world today, people are always coming and going. I'll get close to someone
only to have her swept away to California, or New York, or Iowa. On good
days I can appreciate that I have friends in just about every state in the
USA and several countries abroad. But on the bad days I just feel that
people leave me.

These experiences have contributed to my difficulty allowing some truths to sink into my soul. Truths like, "[Jesus] has said, 'I will never leave you; I will always be by your side'" (Heb. 13:5). Over time He has softened my heart and helped me see His presence in my loneliness; His presence is often quiet and gentle, but undeniable. When I'm lonely, I am learning to tug on the hem of His robe and tell Him what I'm feeling, even though I sometimes feel childish. (Isn't that what He said we should do, anyhow—come to Him like kids?) The beautiful part about being adopted in Christ is that we have every right to "interrupt" the King of the universe. He is the ultimate shelter in the storm. We can rely on Him to be the perfect parent we never had. We can trust Him to nurture us, protect us, and provide for us. He isn't holding out on us. And He will never, ever leave us.

> *We need other believers in our lives who will take an active part in our well-being.*

I hate being lonely. Sometimes there is nothing I loathe more. I've had seasons in my life when I felt absolutely cut off from the rest of the world, invisible in the middle of a crowd. Even God seemed far away. In my efforts to appear strong, I built up walls that would prevent anyone from knowing who I really was. I believed if they really knew, they would run for their lives. Therefore I used the busyness and demands of life to help me push others aside—even those who were reaching out to me. I've learned that times of isolation can keep you longer than you ever wanted to stay.

We all need community. Not a place to go on Sundays, but true community with other followers of Christ. We need other believers in our lives who will take an active part in our well-being. We need them to notice when we're in need and do something about it. We need them to approach us when they're worried about us. We need them to invite us to their children's birthday parties, to bring us food when we're sick or studying for finals, to be with us when we've had a death in the family. As I observe the paths of dear lovers of Jesus, myself included, I see that the road to destruction begins with isolation from other followers of Christ.

Isolation is a slippery slope. Whatever propels you into isolation, at first it seems a little more safe and comfortable; after all, it means you won't get hurt. Or so you think.

You start to get used to no one really knowing what it is that you do with your time. Your friendships become more and more shallow. Before you know it, you've gone weeks or even months without having a meaningful, face-to-face conversation about how you are really doing deep down in your soul. God's soft whisper of a voice gets drowned by thoughts like, *He doesn't really know what's best for me. If He did, I wouldn't be here.* And once this seed of distrust is planted and starts to grow ugly, you look around and don't see anyone who knows how to help you weed it out, or would be willing to help if they did know. So you come to accept it, prickly and thorny and exhausting as it is, and decide to just make the best of this on your own. But what you don't see is that vine of distrust slowly winding itself around you, just waiting to choke the life out of you.

If there's one thing I ask permission to beg of you today, it is this: please don't let yourself stay isolated. All along the way, you always have a choice. I know from experience that it isn't easy to put yourself out there, especially if you are introverted, if you've really been burned by "organized religion," or if you're just plain uncomfortable around people you don't know. And I know how hard it is to be the new guy, the outsider, and even feel sort of like an intruder. But you know what? When you find a group of true followers of Jesus, they'll recognize this because they once were in your spot. And even though it may take a try or two on

> *Whatever propels you into isolation, at first it seems a little more safe and comfortable; after all, it means you won't get hurt. Or so you think.*

your part (they'll be human, too, after all), they'll meet you halfway. Your act of bravery in a terrifying situation will not go unnoticed.

Being in Christ means every one of us is a vital part of the body of Christ. While we each enjoy the same all-access invitation to God, we have unique manifestations of His Spirit within us. Sometimes those gifts are for a season or for one certain situation. Other times they seem to want to burst out of us whether we like it or not. No matter what, these gifts are the Spirit working in and through us to build up the Body of Christ. The Body of Christ encompasses all believers through all time and across cultures, languages, and any other barriers. We have an enormous extended family.

> You are meant to be a part of a local church, and your role is crucial.

At the same time, the body of Christ works in smaller segments throughout the world via local churches. You are meant to be a part of a smaller unit of the body, and your role is crucial. Check out 1 Corinthians 12. Think about it like this: the body of Christ needs you, whether you're a hand, a toe, or a spleen. If you think your presence and involvement in a local church doesn't really matter that much—that you're doing just fine listening to sermons online and praying with a friend—you're really missing out. And the church God might want you to be a part of is missing out, too. If you're disgruntled with your current church because of (fill in the blank) and thinking of leaving, I would ask you to just be sure that it is for a legitimate reason.[2] Otherwise, it is a bit like lopping off a limb and leaving the body to bleed out. Pardon the gory illustration, but I think it's the best way to describe how vital each of us is to our churches whether or not we want to step up to that responsibility.

See, when we're in Christ, we gain a whole posse of brothers and sisters. If you were an only child and always dreamed of having siblings, you're in luck. (If you liked being alone, you'll have some adjusting to do, right?) If you grew up with siblings, as I did, you might have varying reactions. I love my sisters, and I hate that we all live in different parts of the country and don't get to see each other very often. At the same time, oh my goodness, do I remember the fights we had growing up! Being part of a family means we're going to have some conflict along with our connectedness. Things are going to get messy. And really, they should. If you're involved with a small group of believers and you aren't getting into the depths of what is really going on in their lives, you're not experiencing the body of Christ as it is meant to be. You're not really living as the body of Christ. Each member, each "organ" of the body, needs to be fulfilling the role he or she was made for. If God has made you a compassionate person, you need to be listening to people's stories and offering them empathy. If you are constantly reading the Word and feel you might explode if you don't share what you've learned, you may need to be leading a Bible study. The point is this: the Spirit of the living God is within you, working in you to encourage, admonish, challenge, sharpen, and comfort others who are in Christ. I don't know what that will look like for you individually. But I can say with 100 percent confidence that you need to be doing it. Check out what Paul wrote along these lines:

> Because of the grace allotted to me, I can *respectfully* tell you not to think of yourselves as being more important than you are; devote your minds to sound judgment since God has assigned to each of us a measure of faith. For in the same way that one body has so many different parts, each with different functions; we, too—the many—are different parts that form one body in the Anointed One. Each one of us is joined with one another, *and we become together what we could not be alone.* Since our gifts vary depending on the grace poured out on each of us, *it is important that* we exercise the gifts *we have been given.* If prophecy is your gift, then speak as a prophet according to your proportion of faith. If service is your gift, then serve well. If teaching is your gift, then teach well. If you have been given a voice of encouragement, then use it *often.* If giving is your gift, then be generous. If leading, then be eager to get started. If sharing God's mercy, then be cheerful in sharing it.

Love others *well, and* don't hide behind a mask; love authentically. Despise evil; pursue what is good *as if your life depends on it.* Live in true devotion to one another, loving each other as sisters and brothers. Be first to honor others *by putting them first.* Do not slack in your faithfulness and hard work. Let your spirit be on fire, bubbling up and boiling over, as you serve the Lord. *Do not forget to* rejoice, for hope is always just around the corner. Hold up through the hard times that are coming, and devote yourselves to prayer. Share what you have with the saints, so they lack nothing; take every opportunity to open your *life and* home to others.

If people mistreat or malign you, bless them. Always speak blessings, not curses. If some have cause to celebrate, join in the celebration. And if others are weeping, join in that as well. Work toward unity, and live in harmony with one another. Avoid thinking you are better than others or wiser than the rest; instead, embrace common people *and ordinary tasks.* (Rom. 12:3–16)

I love the last bit here—"embrace common people and ordinary tasks." We are each definitely given a unique blend of gifts and talents. But I bet that many of us would say we haven't been gifted with things like cleaning toilets or setting up chairs. Ah, those ordinary tasks! We're quick to pray about whether we should lead a Bible study, but do we pray about whether we should volunteer for Sunday trash duty? Is it any less a sacred moment to serve our brothers and sisters in an undignified task than it is in a lofty one? I think you see where I'm going here. There are some tasks that we need to do in the body of Christ that aren't glamorous, and that, quite honestly, you don't need to sit around waiting for a call from God to do. You're already called to serve. So just do what needs doing when it comes to the little things.

> *ove others well, and* don't hide behind a mask; love authentically.

Now I need to speak a moment to my fellow overachievers. You're the ones who love to say yes to everything. Maybe it is because you think if it's worth doing well, you might as well do it yourself. You've probably had trouble saying no to things your whole life. And you're probably really, really tired all the time. Or maybe that's just me. At any rate, a few years ago I was in the thick of serving my church in lots of different ways, and honestly, I was enjoying it . . . most of the time. We were a small pack of folks, so there weren't a lot of us to go around when it came to most tasks. But as more

You are an important piece in God's kingdom and Christ's Body.

people started joining us, I had a realization: if I was doing all this stuff, they couldn't. My service may have been taking away their opportunity to serve. That was a hard pill to swallow. I have always been one to burn the candle at both ends and in the middle, as my mother would say. So I needed this particular revelation of freedom. I hate feeling like a quitter, so it took all my courage to let the right people know that I needed to take a few steps back. But God honored those steps of obedience, and soon there were new faces doing the activities I had been doing. They had just been waiting for the chance.

Take a moment to reread Romans 12:3–16. Does this sound like a church family you want to be a part of? I know I do. I also know that this kind of church is not a reality for many. Perhaps your church experience has been one that left you a bit burned and turned off altogether. I've been there. I want to encourage you to not give up and to keep an open heart to what God has for you. I think it's pretty clear through all we've read that God doesn't mean for any of us to be on our own. Remember that you are needed just as much as you need a community of faith. You are an important piece in God's kingdom and Christ's Body. Maybe you're in a part of the country or world that is in desperate need of a community of faith like we've been describing. Could it be that God is calling you to start that church and meet a need by gathering together a few other believers? Or maybe you live in an area that has a church on every corner, and you're having a difficult time finding "the one." My advice is to pray for God to

make it clear which church family you are supposed to be a part of, where you can use your gifts to build up that community. Once that happens, go all in and don't look back.

The Early Church

The first group of Christians, before they were even called "Christians," were a tight-knit group, even though there were thousands of them. A common bond of love for Jesus held them together and overflowed into love for one another. This didn't mean they never experienced internal conflict (the early chapters of Acts definitely show us otherwise). But they shared a kindred Spirit that went far beyond simply shaking hands and saying hello at a worship gathering. Acts 2 and 4 reveal that they shared property, possessions, and finances as a group, caring for one another's physical needs for food, shelter, and so on. They were linked to one another in many areas of life. "And they devoted themselves to the apostles' teaching and the fellowship, to the breaking of bread and the prayers" (Acts 2:42 ESV).

Part of what bound the early church together so strongly was the fact that they were so vehemently opposed by others. Their leaders were often arrested, held in prison, put on trial, and beaten within an inch of their lives. This is something that we in the United States can't fully appreciate at this point in our history, but it occurs daily in other parts of the world, especially for pastors and other church leaders in those other parts.

The first Christians were incredibly brave. After Peter and John had been arrested and questioned, what was the larger group's response? They prayed:

> "And now, Lord, look upon their threats and grant to your servants to continue to speak your word with all boldness, while you stretch out your hand to heal, and signs and wonders are performed through the name of your holy servant Jesus." And when they had prayed, the place in which they were gathered together was shaken, and they were

all filled with the Holy Spirit and continued to speak the word of God with boldness. (Acts 4:29–31 ESV)

They sought not safety from problems, but courage to minister.

In Christ, we have a responsibility to one another that will stretch our resources to the limit at times, whether or not those are tangible resources. In fact, if we aren't feeling a bit of a pinch, perhaps we are wise to ask ourselves whether we are as intimately connected to other believers as God wants us to be. Are we involved enough in one another's lives to be aware of the basic needs that exist in our local body of faith?

vv. 1–13

CONTEXT:

Read Romans 14 to get the context for this chapter. Paul had been urging believers to put others' needs before their own and to recognize that not everybody is at the same place in their journey of faith.

omans 15

vv. 1–3

STANDOUT MOMENTS:

In Christ, we no longer have to be concerned with keeping up our reputations to look good. Instead, we are free to seek the welfare of others for God's glory and their sake.

¹ *So now what?* We who are strong are not just to satisfy our own desires. We are called to carry the weaknesses of those who are not strong. ² Each of us must strive to please our neighbors, pursuing their welfare so they will become strong. ³ The Anointed One Himself *is our model for this kind of living,* for He did not live to please Himself. And as the Scriptures declared, "When they insult You, they insult me." ⁴ You see, everything written in

the days of old was recorded to give us instructions *for living*. We find encouragement through the Scriptures and a call to perseverance that will produce hopeful living. [5] I pray that our God, who calls you and gives you perseverance and encouragement, will join all of you together to share one mind according to Jesus the Anointed. [6] In this unity, you will share one voice as you glorify *the one True* God, the Father of our Lord Jesus, the Anointed One, *our Liberating King.*

[7] So accept one another in the same way the Anointed has accepted you so that God will get the praise He is due. [8] For, as I am *fond of* saying, the Anointed One has become a servant of the Jews in order to demonstrate God's truth. Effectively this confirms the promises He made to our ancestors [9] and causes the non-Jewish nations to glorify God for His mercy. As the Scriptures say,

> For this I will praise You among the nations
>   and sing praises to Your name.

[10] Again the Scriptures say,

> Nations, celebrate with His *covenant* people

[11] And again,

> Praise the Lord, all nations.
>   Raise your voices, all people; let your praises flow to God.

[12] Again Isaiah says,

> Then, the root of Jesse will emerge—
>   He rises to rule all the peoples of the world
> *who come to Him for guidance and direction.*
>   In Him they place their hope.

vv. 6–7

BIG PICTURE:

Check out John 17, part of Jesus' prayer the night before He died.

vv. 9–12

ORIGINAL AUDIENCE:

If any of the non-Jewish believers at the time were questioning whether it was God's plan to include them in the Body of Christ, these verses from the Old Testament must have been very encouraging. It was always part of God's ultimate rescue plan to include people from every nation.

¹³ I pray that God, the source of all hope, will infuse your lives with an abundance of joy and peace in the midst of your faith so that your hope will overflow through the power of the Holy Spirit.

v. 13

PRAYER:

Father, You are a God of hope, not despair! Let Your Spirit of peace and joy permeate our hearts and fill us to overflowing, so that a dying world can find life in You.

PRAYER

BIG PICTURE

CONTEXT

ORIGINAL AUDIENCE

STAND OUT MOMENTS

Come Together

❈ When have you felt the most vulnerable and alone, as though there was no one to take care of you?

❈ When have you felt you most belonged?

❈ In what ways has God gifted and called you to serve the Body of Christ and your local church specifically? (If you aren't aware of your spiritual gifts or the current needs in your church, take some time to discuss together how you might discover them.)

❈ Share a "Standout Moment" from this chapter and what you will do as a result.

Notes

NOW...

But Not Yet

For this perishable body must put on the imperishable,
and this mortal body must put on immortality.

—1 Corinthians 15:53 (ESV)

CHAPTER EIGHT

DWELLING Occupied

Home is the place where, when you
   have to go there,

They have to take you in.

I should have called it

Something you somehow haven't to
   deserve.

—Robert Frost,
   "The Death of the Hired Man" [1]

In Christ, I am . . . God's dwelling place

In Christ, you are . . . God's dwelling place.

God did something the law could never do. *You see, human flesh took its toll on God's law. In and of itself, the law is not weak; but* the flesh weakens it. So to condemn the sin that was *ruling* in the flesh, God sent His own Son, bearing the likeness of sinful flesh, as a sin offering. Now we are able to live up to the justice demanded by the law. But that ability has not come from living by our fallen human nature; it has

come because we walk according to the movement of the Spirit in our lives. (Romans 8:3–4)

One of my favorite travel experiences took place in the middle of nowhere in a small village in the mountains of Southeast Asia. The village had no running water, very little electricity, and spiders the size of my hand. The people were some of the happiest and most welcoming I'd ever encountered.

One night, my team and I were sitting in the dark with the village elders sharing stories about God's goodness and singing hymns. I'll never forget the feeling I had as we sang "How Great Thou Art" simultaneously in three languages: Korean, Thai, and English. Our voices mixed with the nighttime mountain sounds as all of creation lifted its song to the heavens.

What is the kingdom of God? In that moment, I felt it was right there with me. But it can still be easy to get caught up in thinking of the kingdom as some far-off place I'll experience someday in heaven. While there is absolutely a vital, future aspect, we need to be aware that the kingdom of God is here and now too. Jesus taught it time and again: "Repent, for the kingdom of heaven is at hand" (Matt. 3:2 NASB). "The time is fulfilled, and the kingdom of God is at hand; repent and believe in the gospel" (Mark 1:15 ESV). "Behold, the kingdom of God is in your midst" (Luke 17:21 NASB). The term *at hand* can be defined as "to bring near, to join one thing to another; to draw or come near to, to approach."[2] The Kingdom is among us. It is both here and not yet.

The defining characteristic of God's kingdom is always the same: His presence. His Spirit. His dwelling among His people. Where God is present, He is King. And since He is present everywhere at all times, He is King everywhere at all times. The indwelling Spirit is what makes us citizens of His Kingdom, what transforms us into His living Temple, and what gives us the work of priests. These are potentially heavy concepts that require some digging into their context from the Old Testament, so let's investigate some of that now.

What makes people a part of God's kingdom? His presence with them. Citizens of God's kingdom exist throughout time and space but look different depending on which side of history they live or lived—before Jesus or after Jesus. Because of the fallen nature of the world and sin within humans, in the Old Testament people's interaction with Him was limited and, as it still is today, entirely dependent on God's initiation of communication and contact. God knew the people needed a representation of His presence that they could see and touch—physical symbols that reflected a spiritual reality. Thus throughout the Old Testament He gave them a pillar of smoke, a cloud, a burning bush, an ornate gold box. He was making provisions for their need, meeting them where they were. His presence, power, and rule were not limited by these physical representations; in fact, the opposite was true: He was holding back for the people's benefit. They experienced as much of God as He knew they could handle. God has always been the supreme example of selflessness. He temporarily set aside His glory to bring us to Himself, to re-create His original purposes for us, to draw us into communion with Him.

One of my favorite words is *shekinah*. The concept of *shekinah* is found throughout the Old and New Testaments, although the word itself ("the one who dwells, that which dwells") is not.[3] It refers to the glorious presence of God, and more specifically, a visible sign of God's presence.[4] Rabbinic literature views the pillars of fire and smoke in Exodus especially as *shekinah* glory, physical manifestations of God's presence.

Have you ever had a moment when God's presence was so real to you, you felt as if He were almost physically present? What was that like?

Most people are probably familiar with the ark of the covenant, even if only via pop culture or TV shows. It is always shrouded in mystery, isn't it? In the Old Testament, God's presence was not confined to the ark of the covenant, but the ark was still extremely significant in communicating that He was Israel's God. God gave Moses instructions for building the ark of the covenant and the tabernacle, a type of portable worship center (see Exodus 25–27). The ark, a beautifully crafted wooden chest overlaid with gold, sat in the most holy place of the tabernacle, called the Holy of Holies. The ark's cover, which was topped with two golden angels, was referred to as the *mercy seat*, or place of atonement. God's presence would rest on the mercy seat. The ark contained the tablets of the Ten Commandments and was sprinkled with sacrificial blood each year by the high priest on the Day of Atonement to cleanse the people of sin. It was where God met with Moses. Additionally, the ark was carried before the Israelites in battle. "And whenever the ark set out, Moses said, 'Arise, O LORD, and let your enemies be scattered, and let those who hate you flee before you.' And when it rested, he said, 'Return, O LORD, to the ten thousand thousands of Israel'" (Num. 10:35–36 ESV).

The defining characteristic of God's kingdom is always the same: His presence.

Other nations throughout the Old Testament recognized the importance and power of the ark. First Samuel 4–6 recounts a dark time in Israel's history when the ark was stolen by their adversaries the Philistines. Israel suffered a major defeat that day—not only in battle, but in that the very presence of God had been taken away by their enemies. The people of Israel were bereft. However, instead of experiencing victory, the Philistines suffered numerous plague-like illnesses while they possessed the ark. They passed it from town to town, even placing it in one of their own pagan temples, in an attempt to rid themselves of its effects. The statue of their god kept toppling over facedown in front of the ark, its hands and head even breaking off. The Philistines soon recognized that it wasn't the ark itself that possessed power, but God: "When the men of Ashdod saw what was happening, they said, 'The ark of Israel's God must not stay here with us, because His hand is strongly against us and our god Dagon'" (1 Sam. 5:7 HCSB). Finally the Philistines gave up and sent the ark back to Israel.

Much as the ark did, the tabernacle served as another physical representation of spiritual reality. Its construction, ornamentation, and the articles within it were essential to the sacrificial system, and thus the people's relationship with God. Priests assisted in making continual animal sacrifices on behalf of the people so they could all be in right standing with Him. But as we've already covered, the sacrificial system didn't fully cleanse the guilt in a person's heart—there was always another reason to have to sacrifice again.

Long after Moses led the people of Israel, King David recognized the beauty and weight of the mercy seat and wanted to build a more permanent house for God. David did much to prepare for the Temple, but it was his son King Solomon who eventually built it after David's death. Hundreds of years passed, and eventually the Temple was destroyed and God's people were exiled. After many years they returned to Jerusalem to rebuild the Temple, but even with King Herod's later, lavish reconstruction, it was never quite the same. This was the Temple of Jesus' day.

> The Word became flesh
> and took up residence among us.
> We observed His glory,
> the glory as the One and Only Son from the Father,
> full of grace and truth. (John 1:14 HCSB)

The Word became flesh. Jesus embodied the presence of God because He was and is God. The Greek for "took up residence among us" could be literally translated "tabernacled among us." Jesus set up camp in the midst of His people. Jesus was the ultimate *shekinah*, the full representation of

God in flesh (see Colossians 1:19; 2:9). While the people were keeping an eye out for a military figure to bring freedom, Jesus came as something far better—God in the flesh, the Liberating King. He established a new era in an eternal kingdom without borders. It is this kingdom of which we who are in Christ are a part.

The Gospels recount Jesus' spending much time describing the kingdom of God via dozens of parables. Parables are stories that, though the details may be fictional, communicate truth (Matt. 13:11–17, 34–35). There is a passage that stands out in my mind for our purposes of identity: "The kingdom of heaven is like treasure hidden in a field, which a man found and covered up. Then in his joy he goes and sells all that he has and buys that field. Again, the kingdom of heaven is like a merchant in search of fine pearls, who, on finding one pearl of great value, went and sold all that he had and bought it" (Matt. 13:44–46 ESV).

In the first part of the story, the kingdom is compared to buried treasure. In the second, it is compared to a merchant. In the first part of the story, the kingdom is what is sought and found; in the second part, the kingdom is doing the seeking. I find it fascinating that even though God is sovereign and the One who initiates everything with us, our relationship with Him always goes both ways. We seek Him only because He first sought us. You see, in the second part of this story, the One seeking sells everything He has to purchase the expensive pearl. Friends, we are that "pearl of great price." Christ's kingdom is infinitely more valuable than we can ever fathom, and we seek it above all else because we love Him, and He is worth our abandoning everything else we might have. When we recognize the value of being a part of God's kingdom, we will leave everything else behind. It's an incredible exchange, except that our perceived sacrifice is paltry compared to what He gave for us. God finds us valuable and hasn't ever regretted what it cost Him to rescue us.

The whole earth sprouts *newness and life in the springtime,*

and green shoots break through the well-seeded garden soil.

That's what it is like with the Eternal's *victory—*

the Lord will cause justice and praise to sprout up before all the nations, *for all peoples to see.* (Isa. 61:11)

Let's take another, deeper look at the Temple and the activity of the priests who served there. Religion professors K. C. Hanson and Douglas Oakman point out that in contrast to our culture's individualistic approach to religion, first-century Palestine and other ancient cultures were quite different. "Not only were 'church and state' not separated in such societies, . . . Religious institutions, as all political life generally, were divided by personal factions striving to occupy the key positions of benefit from the religious system; participation happened through the group and was relatively impersonal."[5] The Temple standing at this time was the second Temple, built during the rule of Persia (520 BC) and later elaborately remodeled by Herod the Great (20 BC). The people had to pay taxes for it on a continual basis. As such, the Temple served as a type of bank and warehouse as well as a center for religious activity.

The Temple was run by priestly families, and during Jesus' time the high priests were appointed by Rome. The priests that served under the high priests oversaw various areas of life, maintaining order not only over ritual and judicial aspects, but also over administrative and economic.[6] Priests held positions such as accountants, scribes, singers, gatekeepers, lawyers, and police. To qualify as a high priest in Jesus' time, a man would have to be part of one of four elite priestly families. The rest of the priests were selected from a group of twenty-four priestly families,[7] and they served throughout the year, a week at a time (Luke 1:8–9). Hanson and

Oakman reveal, "Altogether, there may have been as many as fifteen hundred priests available for the weekly services"[8] at the Temple. Priests had much to gain from their work, both spiritually and economically. Because of all this, it was common for priests in Jesus' time to exploit others, especially peasants, for personal gain.

> Jesus fulfilled every requirement of the Temple sacrifice system and was the final offering for sin.

Jesus had very harsh words for this elitist mentality that had come to define the Temple of that day (see Matthew 23). Recall His indignation at the way people were extorted and how God's house of prayer had become a marketplace (John 2:13–22).

While Temple worship was largely segregated, Jesus' sacrifice opened God's kingdom to all people of all nations. Upon His atoning death, the thick veil separating the Holy of Holies from the rest of the Temple (and the world) was torn from top to bottom (Matt. 27:50–51), showing that there was no longer any barrier standing in the way between God and humanity (Heb. 10:19–20). There was no longer a need for a high priest to offer sacrifices; Jesus is now the perfect High Priest (Heb. 4:14–16). Jesus fulfilled every requirement of the Temple sacrifice system and was the final offering for sin. Jesus as God in the flesh was King on Earth, both Priest and Sacrifice.

So, when the New Testament writers mentioned that we as Jesus' followers, as citizens of the kingdom and children of God, are a holy, royal priesthood, what might they have had in mind? Surely they had in mind the original role of priest, which in the Old Testament was pictured as a set-apart servant of God and servant of the people, making intercession and assisting in communion with God. The idea of being chosen and set apart for a Holy Spirit–empowered purpose comes to light as we read Paul's words: "*His grace makes me who* I am, a minister of the Anointed One, Jesus, called to serve the nations. The good news of God is the focus of my priestly work. In effect, these nations have become an offering to

God, totally acceptable, indeed made holy by the work of the Holy Spirit" (Rom. 15:16). And Peter's words are probably the best known when it comes to our identity as priests:

> Come to Him—the living stone—who was rejected by people but *accepted* by God as chosen and precious. Like living stones, let yourselves be assembled into a spiritual house, a holy order of priests who offer up spiritual sacrifices that will be acceptable to God through Jesus the Anointed . . . But you are a chosen people, *set aside to be* a royal order of priests, a holy nation, God's own; so that you may proclaim the wondrous acts of the One who called you out of *inky* darkness into shimmering light. Once you were not a people, but now you are God's people; once you had not received mercy, but now you have received it. (1 Peter 2:4–5, 9–10)

Imagine the excitement this must have brought Peter's original audience! In Christ, there was no need to bury yourself in endless genealogies to prove your worth because of your family line. In fact, even if you were a Gentile, you had a place in His family. No need to feel overlooked when it came to important tasks. There was no politically charged high priest lording over you; Jesus Christ Himself is the High Priest. And even if tangible wealth was evasive, your spiritual wealth was beyond compare. The same is true for us: in Christ, we are chosen, set apart, and made holy (1 Peter 2:9), offering ourselves as living sacrifices (Rom. 12:1) to intercede for others and bring them to Him (2 Cor. 5:18–20).

★ ★ ★

Life for first-century followers of Jesus was quite volatile. Believers lived in a culture that was rife with political oppression and racial tension, to put it lightly. This is partially why Jesus' disciples were hoping He was going to establish a physical kingdom by overthrowing the Roman government—to restore not only their nation politically but to eradicate harmful Gentile influence as a whole. Jews and non-Jews were locked in constant, heated opposition on every level of society. Christ-following Jews were shunned

by their families because in general the Jewish community rejected the notion that Jesus was Messiah. The people of Jesus' day were on the lookout for a military figure to set them free from Rome, but Jesus instead established a spiritual kingdom without borders. Then Gentiles began joining the family of God through Christ. Can you imagine what kind of uproar this caused? Paul wrote to encourage non-Jewish Christians but to also remind them of the weight of their inclusion into the Kingdom:

> So never forget how you used to be. Those of you born as outsiders *to Israel* were *outcasts*, branded "the uncircumcised" by those who bore the sign of the covenant in their flesh, a sign made with human hands. You had absolutely no connection to the Anointed; you were strangers, separated from God's people. You were aliens to the covenant they had with God; you were hopelessly stranded without God in a *fractured* world. But now, because of Jesus the Anointed *and His sacrifice, all of that has changed.* God gathered you who were so far away and brought you near to Him by the *royal* blood of the Anointed, *our Liberating King . . .* (Eph. 2:11–13).

> The Great Preacher of peace *and love* came for you, and *His voice* found those of you who were near and those who were far away. By Him both have access to the Father in one Spirit. And so you are no longer called outcasts and wanderers but citizens with God's people, *members of God's holy family,* and residents of His household. You are being built on a *solid* foundation: *the message* of the prophets and *the voices* of God's chosen emissaries with Jesus, the Anointed Himself, the *precious* cornerstone. The building is joined together *stone by stone—all of us chosen and sealed* in Him, rising up to become a holy temple in the Lord. In Him you are being built together, creating a *sacred* dwelling place *among you* where God can live in the Spirit. (Eph. 17–22)

I love this imagery. Though we were once wanderers, we now have a home in Christ. Though we were once outcasts, now we have a family in Christ. Though we were once nobodies, now we are special in Christ. Built on His strong foundation, we come together as His Body to make up a living house for His Spirit and are now priests who live to bring other wanderers and outcasts to Him.

> The building is joined together *stone by stone—all of us chosen and sealed* in Him, rising up to become a holy temple in the Lord. In Him you are being built together, creating a *sacred* dwelling place *among you* where God can live in the Spirit. (Eph. 2:21–22)

> All these I have mentioned died in faith without receiving the full promises, although they saw the fulfillment as though from a distance. These people accepted and confessed that they were strangers and foreigners on this earth because people who speak like this make it plain that they are still seeking a homeland. If this was only a bit of nostalgia for a time and place they left behind, then certainly they might have turned around and returned. But such saints as these look forward to a far better place, a heavenly country. So God is not ashamed to be called their God because He has prepared a *heavenly* city for them. (Heb. 11:13–16)

Even when God's people had their own land, they looked forward to a time and place that was in the future. The physical land of Israel, or promised land, is not necessarily what God had in mind as the kingdom of God . . . The United States of America is not the kingdom of God . . . the kingdom of God is not of this world, even though many of its inhabitants are on this earthly soil.

Now we are citizens of God's kingdom; His eternal spiritual kingdom exists at the same time as the temporal physical nation in which we live. Human political lines are nonexistent in God's kingdom but must be recognized while we live in this reality. As we've covered, we are to operate within the laws of our land, and may at times need to leverage politics of the world for kingdom purposes. But our loyalty is to God's kingdom, over patriotism. If your politics get you more worked up than your love for Jesus and following in His ways, that's a problem. Instead, since we are "strangers and foreigners on this earth," let's encourage one another to

keep our eyes on the future fulfillment of our citizenship in the kingdom. After His resurrection, why didn't Jesus just stay here? Why did He ascend to the heavenly realm of His Kingdom? Jesus told us that it was to our benefit that He return to Heaven because God was sending His Spirit to reside in human hearts. Though God had told Moses, "You cannot see My face, for no one can see Me and live" (Ex. 33:20 HCSB), Jesus was God in flesh, and He mercifully walked the earth without striking dead every person with whom He came into contact. But haven't we who are in Christ died to ourselves, died to sin, died because we recognized the severity of our situation apart from Jesus and His loving redemption? Because we have been crucified with Christ (Gal. 2:20) and it is He who gives us new life, breath, and being (Acts 17:28), we are not only living stones that make up a temple not made with human hands, but we are also the face of God to the world, the physical representations of a spiritual reality. Without a doubt God still works in ways that don't require our participation. But as His living "temples," our lives are constant, living, breathing symbols of His grand rescue plan for all the world. We can experience His *shekinah* daily.

As His living "temples," our lives are constant, living, breathing symbols of His grand rescue plan for all the world.

Ruth

Ruth was a Gentile woman living in Moab during the Old Testament time before Israel had a king. She lived with her mother-in-law, Naomi, and both Ruth's and Naomi's husbands had passed away. Ruth's father-in-law, Elimelech, was originally from Bethlehem and had died before she married into the family. Naomi planned to return to the land of Judah, having heard that the famine that had originally led her to Moab was over. Ruth no longer had any obligations to this family, since Naomi had no other sons for her to marry (the practice at the time), but she chose to go with Naomi to Israel anyway. Ruth told Naomi, "Wherever you go, I will go. Wherever you live, I will live. Your people will be my people. Your God will be my God. Wherever you die, I will also die and be buried there near you. May the Eternal One punish me—and even more so—if anything besides death comes between us" (Ruth 1:17).

Ruth packed up and left the only home and country she had ever known. She trusted in the God of Israel to provide for their needs and safety along the journey, and He certainly did. The political climate between Moab and Israel was interesting. On one hand, Israel regarded Moab as relatives (Gen. 19:30–38), but on the other, they definitely had conflict (Judg. 3:12–30). Ruth and Naomi traveled during a time of peace between the two nations, although the Israelites likely did not think very highly of Moabites in general. Eventually God provided Ruth with a husband from Elimelech's family, a man named Boaz, and her story concludes with the awesome reveal that she was King David's great-grandmother.

Ruth's life and story could have ended much differently; she was an outsider and easily could have been despised because of her nationality. She could have faded into an unremarkable history. But God had other plans. He chose Ruth to play a pivotal part in His kingdom, the lineage of King David, and more important, the lineage of the Messiah. She is mentioned by name in Matthew's genealogy of Jesus (Matt.1:5). An outsider became a part of God's people and His story. A foreigner became a part of the nation of Israel. And so it is with us.

God accepts people no matter where they come from or who their parents are or what color their skin might be. God's kingdom is open to all who trust in Christ. Every tribe, nation, and tongue. There are no racial, economic, or political lines in God's kingdom. While God is already King, there are those who have yet to know this. One day every knee will bow to Him, but how much sweeter that day will be for those who worship Him willingly today! His desire is for all of us to be in His presence forever.

Step into the Story

Be sure to read all of Romans 11 before you dive into the selections here.

Romans 11:1–5, 13–17, 25–36

¹ Now I ask you, has God rejected His people? Absolutely not! *I'm living proof that God is faithful.* I am an Israelite, Abraham's my father, and Benjamin's my tribe. ² God has not, *and will not,* abandon His covenant people; He always knew they would belong to Him. Don't you remember the story of what happens when Elijah pleads with God to deal with Israel? The Scripture tells us *his protest:* ³ "Lord, they have murdered Your prophets, they have demolished Your altars, and I alone am left *faithful to You*; now they are seeking to kill me." ⁴ How does God answer his pleas for help? He says, "I have held back 7,000 men who are faithful to Me; none have bowed a knee to worship Baal."

⁵ The same thing is happening now. God has preserved a remnant, elected by grace. ⁶ Grace *is central in God's action here, and it* has nothing to do with deeds prescribed by the law. If it did, grace would not be grace.

vv. 1–5

BIG PICTURE:

Check out 1 Kings 19 for the backstory here.

v. 6

PRAYER:

Father, thank You for the grace You have given us in Christ. Help me to know what it means to be a part of the remnant that is faithful to You.

¹³ But I have this to say to all of you who are not ethnic Jews: I am God's emissary to you, and I honor this call by focusing on what God is doing with and through you. ¹⁴ I do this so that somehow my own blood brothers and sisters will be made jealous; and that, I trust, will bring some to salvation. ¹⁵ If the fact that they are currently set aside resolves the hostility between God and the rest of the world, what will their acceptance bring if not life from the dead? ¹⁶ If the first and best of the dough you offer is sacred, the entire loaf will be as well. If the root of the tree is sacred, the branches will be also.

vv. 17–18

ORIGINAL AUDIENCE:

Paul was writing to Gentile believers here. It could have been easy for them to get a prideful, "us versus them" mentality about having God's favor. Paul warned them to remember their roots; Jesus Himself was born a Jew, after all.

¹⁷ Imagine some branches are cut off *of the cultivated olive tree* and other branches of a wild olive (which represents all of you *outsiders*) are grafted in their place. You are nourished by the root of the *cultivated* olive tree. ¹⁸ It doesn't give you license to become proud and self-righteous about the fact that you've been grafted in. If you do boast, remember that the branches do not sustain the root—it is the system of roots that *nourishes and* supports you.

vv. 25–29

STANDOUT MOMENTS:

God is always, always faithful. He doesn't go back on His promises. He will keep promises He made thousands and thousands of years ago. My relationship with God is interwoven across time and space with others who have seen His faithfulness.

²⁵ My brothers and sisters, I do not want you to be in the dark about this mystery—*I am going to let you in on the plan* so that you will not think too highly of yourselves. A part of Israel has been hardened *to the good news* until the full number of those outside the Jewish family have entered in. ²⁶ This is the way that all of Israel will be saved. As it was written, *so it also stands:*

The Deliverer will come from Zion;

He will drive away wickedness from Jacob.

27 And this is My covenant promise to them,

on the day when I take away their sins.

28 *It may seem strange.* When it comes to *the work of* the gospel, the fact that they oppose it is actually for your benefit. But when you factor in God's election, they are truly loved because they descended from faithful forefathers. 29 You see, when God gives a *grace* gift and issues a call *to a people*, He does not change His mind and take it back. 30 There was a time when you *outsiders* were disobedient to God *and at odds with His purpose*, but now you have experienced mercy as a result of their disobedience. 31 In the same way, their disobedience now will make a way for them to receive mercy as a result of the mercy shown to you. 32 For God has assigned all of us together—*Jews and non-Jews, insiders and outsiders*—to disobedience so He can show His mercy to all. 33 *We cannot wrap our minds around* God's wisdom and knowledge! Its depths can never be measured! We cannot understand His judgments or explain the mysterious ways that He works! For,

34 Who can fathom the mind of the Lord?

Or who can claim to be His advisor?

35 Or,

Who can give to God in advance

so that God must pay him back?

36 For all that exists originates in Him, comes through Him, and is moving toward Him; so give Him the glory forever. Amen.

vv. 30–32

CONTEXT:

Just as Gentiles are rescued through Christ, Jews are rescued through Christ. God shows His mercy to all people without distinction. However, "all" doesn't mean that every single person is shown mercy (aka universalism); Paul taught that only those who trust Christ for salvation will be shown mercy. So this is "all" as in "any," not "every."

 **PRAYER**

 **BIG PICTURE**

 **CONTEXT**

 **ORIGINAL AUDIENCE**

 **STAND OUT MOMENTS**

Come Together

❊ What does it mean to be a part of God's kingdom here and now? What might it look like to be a part of God's kingdom to come?

❊ In what ways do you sacrifice on behalf of others? What does it look like to lay aside our rights for the sake of others?

❊ What does it look like to intercede for those who don't believe?

❊ Share a "Standout Moment" from this chapter and what you will do as a result.

"My kingdom is not recognized in this world. If this were My kingdom, My servants would be fighting for My freedom. But My kingdom is not in this physical realm."

—John 18:36

Notes

CHAPTER NINE

WORSHIPER

Fulfilled

> Thou hast made us for Thyself
>
> And our hearts are restless until they rest
>   in Thee.
> —St. Augustine

In Christ, I am . . . fulfilled.

In Christ, you are . . . a worshiper.

If you live your life animated by the flesh—*namely, your fallen, corrupt nature*—then your mind is focused on the matters of the flesh. But if you live your life animated by the Spirit—*namely, God's indwelling presence*—then your focus is on the work of the Spirit. A mind focused on the flesh is doomed to death, but a mind focused on the Spirit will find full life and complete peace. You see, a mind focused on the flesh is declaring war against God; it defies the authority of God's law and is incapable of following His path. *So it is clear that* God takes no pleasure in those who live oriented to the flesh. (Rom. 8:5–8)

There are some of us who would never categorize ourselves as addicts. Certainly some of us genuinely do struggle with addictions that we're all familiar with—alcohol, drugs, food, sex. What about those of us who haven't yet come to grips with the fact that we, too, are addicted, but to things like approval, admiration, success, or control?

> A mind focused on the flesh is doomed to death, but a mind focused on the Spirit will find full life and complete peace.

God wired us with certain needs that are universal and healthy. In American culture to be labeled "needy" is the ultimate put-down. But God created us to need. We all need physical elements, like air, food, and water. We need autonomy, and yet we also need interdependence. We need to be able to express ourselves creatively, to know we are worth something, and even to laugh. We will either find a way to fulfill these needs one way or another, or we will get so used to being unfulfilled that parts of us wither up and die. Morbid, I know. But true.

In my struggles with depression, my worst times are usually when I've been ignoring some real need I have. There have been huge chunks of my life that I spent depressed because I didn't know I was depressed and didn't realize there was another way to live. There have been other chunks of life that I spent depressed simply because the feeling was familiar.

Getting our needs fulfilled is tricky. Many of us never stop to think about our invisible needs or those of others. We are just trying to make it through the day, right? And for some of us, when we express these invisible needs and are looking for healthy ways to fill them, we don't get what we really need. This could be because we don't know how to adequately express our needs. It could be because we do express our needs, but to people who aren't equipped to help us fill them. It could also be because we find ways that seem to fill the need at the time but actually aren't fulfilling at all in the end.

Enter addiction. Every now and then we stumble upon something that seems to make us feel *good*—so good that we don't ever want to feel "ungood" again. The disappointing thing is that the good feeling often disappears way too quickly. The new pair of shoes. The control we had in that meeting with coworkers. The extra dessert. The way she acted when I put her in her place. The third beer. The new smartphone. The new boyfriend.

Or . . . going to church twice on a Sunday because I "have" to. Volunteering so I can look awesome to others. Going to my third Bible study in a week so I can feel holy.

It's never enough, is it? Is this what Jesus was talking about when He promised us life abundant? Or is it veiled idolatry?

Even when we look to "positive" things to fill certain needs, they can come up short in fulfilling us. My theory is that our needs each have their own corresponding fulfillments. (Can we all say a big "duh" together?) If I need support for a recent decision I made, going on a wilderness journey by myself isn't going to fulfill that need. If I need to mourn a loss, going to a bunch of parties to forget about it won't help me. If I need empathy for hard stuff I'm going through, eating a tub of ice cream won't satisfy me. The idea of looking in the right places for fulfillment seems really, really simple . . . but if it were so simple in practice, I think I would live a much more fulfilled life.

A question I've heard many times is, "Doesn't God just want me to be happy?" Well, yes. I do think God wants us to be happy, as in joyfully fulfilled. I also think He wants us to have joy that transcends circumstances. That kind of fulfillment can only come from a deep-rooted sense of security in Jesus. Psalm 16:11 (NASB) says, "You will make known to me the path of life; in Your presence is fullness of joy; in Your right hand there are pleasures forever." That definitely tells me that God

> *Is this what Jesus was talking about when He promised us life abundant? Or is it veiled idolatry?*

is concerned with our happiness. "It would seem that Our Lord finds our desires not too strong, but too weak. We are half-hearted creatures, fooling about with drink and sex and ambition when infinite joy is offered us, like an ignorant child who wants to go on making mud pies in a slum because he cannot imagine what is meant by the offer of a holiday at the sea. We are far too easily pleased."[1] Nothing will ever be as satisfying to us as God Himself.

> *Our definition of happiness and the things that we find attractive change over time as we find more of our fulfillment and security in Jesus.*

Our definition of happiness and the things that we find attractive change over time as we find more of our fulfillment and security in Jesus. Just as our taste buds change as time goes by, the "taste buds" of our hearts change as we grow into who we are meant to be. When we've allowed our identity in Christ to inform our everyday decisions, we will eventually find that certain things may no longer excite us. Lesser pleasures aren't as enticing as they once were. We won't default to the same old habits as often as we once did. While this side of eternity we will always have to fight against sin, hopefully we will have moments when we will be able to look back on the past and see that growth has occurred. We will be able to see that what now bring us joy also brings God joy. We will begin to dream God's dreams rather than coming up with our own plans and asking Him to bless them. And the cool thing is that all this change in us tends to happen slowly and often goes unnoticed without much fanfare. It's one of those times we realize in hindsight. I think that's how we can tell it is authentic—when we've occupied ourselves with loving Jesus so much that we don't even notice that we've begun to love the lesser things . . . well, less.

Jesus: I tell you the truth: the man who crawls through the fence of the sheep pen, rather than walking through the gate, is a thief or a vandal. The shepherd walks openly through the entrance. The guard who is posted to protect the sheep opens the gate for the shepherd, and the sheep hear his voice. He calls his own sheep by name and leads them out. When all the sheep have been gathered, he walks on ahead of them; and they follow him because they know his voice. The sheep would not be willing to follow a stranger; they run because they do not know the voice of a stranger.

Jesus explained a profound truth through this metaphor, but they did not understand His teaching. So He explained further.

Jesus: I tell you the truth: I am the gate of the sheep. All who approached the sheep before Me came as thieves and robbers, and the sheep did not listen to their voices. I am the gate; whoever enters through Me will be liberated, will go in and go out, and will find pastures. The thief approaches *with malicious intent*, looking to steal, slaughter, and destroy; I came to give life with joy and abundance.

I am the good shepherd. The good shepherd lays down His life for the sheep *in His care*. The hired hand is not like the shepherd caring for His own sheep. When a wolf attacks, snatching and scattering the sheep, he runs for his life, leaving them *defenseless*. The hired hand runs because he works only for wages and does not care for the sheep. I am the good shepherd; I know My sheep, and My sheep know Me. As the Father knows Me, I know the Father; I will give My life for the sheep. There are many more sheep than you can see here, and I will bring them as well. They will hear My voice, and the flock will be united. One flock. One shepherd. The Father loves Me because I *am willing to* lay down My life—but I will take it up again. My life cannot be taken away by anybody else; I am giving it of My own free will. My authority allows Me to give My life and to take it again. All this has been commanded by My Father. (John 10:1–18)

Jesus described Himself as a shepherd and His followers like sheep. I'm a city girl, so I didn't grow up around many farm animals. But everything I've always heard about them is that they are kind of dumb. I have to stick up for our woolly little friends here. If they're so dumb, why do they follow more faithfully than most humans do? Jesus told us that He is the perfect Shepherd—He leads us into freedom, fulfillment, joy and

abundance. He sees the enemy coming and rises to protect His own. He went so far to protect us that He died for us. And He said that if we're His "sheep," we will know His voice when we hear it and will follow Him. I want to be as gentle as I can here, but this might hurt. If we aren't consistently following Jesus' voice, do we really know what it sounds like? If I'm choosing consistently to go after the lesser things in life, do I really trust Jesus to know what is best for me? If I ignore His voice long enough, how will I recognize it later when I'm about to wander off a cliff and need to hear His guidance? Thankfully, God has ways of getting our attention, but often when we get to the point that He needs to shout, it isn't really all that pleasant. C. S. Lewis wisely said, "We can ignore even pleasure. But pain insists upon being attended to. God whispers to us in our pleasures, speaks in our conscience, but shouts in our pains: it is his megaphone to rouse a deaf world."[2] One of my ongoing prayers is that I will always be so sensitive to God's voice and to the promptings of His Spirit that I am aware of His whispers and will not wander so far that He needs to shout. As we mature in Christ and leave lesser pleasures behind, we will find ourselves more attuned to His voice and find our hearts more full of joy than we could have imagined.

> *So it comes down to this:* since you have been raised with the Anointed One, *the Liberating King*, set your mind on heaven above. The Anointed is there, seated at God's right hand. Stay focused on what's above, not on earthly things, because your *old* life is dead and gone. Your *new* life is now hidden, enmeshed with the Anointed who is in God. On that day when the Anointed One—who is our very life—is revealed, you will be revealed with Him in glory! So kill your earthly impulses: loose sex, impure actions, unbridled sensuality, wicked thoughts, and greed (which is *essentially* idolatry). It's because of these that God's wrath is coming [upon the sons and daughters of disobedience], *so avoid them at all costs.* These are the same things you once pursued, and together you spawned a life of evil. But now make sure you shed such things: anger, rage, spite, slander, and abusive language. And don't go on lying to each other since you have sloughed away your old skin along with

its evil practices for a fresh new you, which is continually renewed in knowledge according to the image of the One who created you. In this re-creation there is no distinction between Greek and Jew, circumcised and uncircumcised, barbarian and conqueror, or slave and free because the Anointed is the whole and dwells in us all. (Col. 3:1–11)

Remember that not only are we in Christ; Christ is in us. There are impulses from our lingering "old selves" that we must continually put to death—impulses of which Christ would never have a part. As God continues to sanctify us internally, our actions will start to reflect Jesus' character more and more. Since we've been made new and "sloughed away our old skin" (Col. 3:9) certain behaviors should disappear, not because we need to earn God's love or our salvation but because we already have God's love and salvation. There is nothing we can do to make Him love us any more or any less. In Christ, it is possible for us to live our lives in a way that radiates the fact that we are deeply and unconditionally loved.

Outside Christ, we are often tempted to seek fulfillment of our needs by turning to idols. Idolatry likely isn't a topic many of us think about on a regular basis. For me, it usually brings to mind a picture of people bowing down to a gold statue. But while bowing in worship of an image of something or someone definitely is idolatry, idolatry takes so many other forms. In a nutshell, I think we can define idolatry as wanting something or someone more than we want God. When I look at idolatry that way, I get a little uncomfortable. Chances are very high that at any given moment I want something more than I want God. I don't think that when we eat because we're hungry or sleep because we're tired that we're guilty of idolatry. Fulfilling our God-given needs in healthy and appropriate God-given ways can actually be a form of worship. When we utilize our abilities, creativity, and talents in ways that honor God, build up others, and energize ourselves, we are worshiping God. But when those avenues of expression become our obsessions, we have crossed a line.

I bet we all know idolatry is sin. And I bet we would like to avoid it! So how do we know when we're allowing something besides God to be our

fuel? We can evaluate our desires and motivations by asking the following questions:

- ❀ What things occupy most of my thoughts? What do I spend the most time thinking about?

- ❀ What do I spend the majority of my time doing?

- ❀ What do I find myself talking about more than anything else?

- ❀ What makes me happier than anything else in the world?

Answers to these questions may not definitively reveal the objects of your worship, but they might give you some hints about whether you are approaching the line of idolatry. Remember that God absolutely blesses us beyond our comprehension in this life, often beyond just the basics for physical life. He gifts us with spiritual blessings and gives us jobs to do on this earth. Those gifts and jobs are part of our worshiping God. What we want to watch out for is becoming obsessed with ourselves, our talents, our abilities, our hobbies, our money, our possessions, and even our family and friends.

If you're realizing something or someone is becoming an idol for you, I recommend talking about it with a trusted friend right away so you can pray about it and discuss an action plan. If your idol is approval from a certain person, the practical ways you handle that are going to be a bit different from how you'd eradicate a hobby idol. So having another strong believer to help you work through the process is important for you to move forward. It may be that you need to take a break from a certain activity or group of people while you regain focus, and perhaps return to that group or activity once your heart is in the right place. Or, it could be that you need to walk away completely and indefinitely. The point is, God is passionate about having all of your worship and devotion. Good gifts can become threats when we allow our affections for them to outgrow our desire for God Himself.

Other roadblocks to our joy being complete in Christ are temptations to stray from following in the ways of Jesus. We are all tempted daily to settle for less than God's best in any given situation. As we discussed earlier, we are going to grapple with temptation as long as we tread this sod. But we can "kill [our] earthly impulses" (Col. 3:5). As we do that, we allow God to form us more into the image of Christ; we allow God to make us look even more like who we really are. Someday, when we pass from this side of eternity into the next, we will experience a new, complete kind of worship in God's presence that we only get little tastes of right now. I don't know about you, but if the joy I experience here is just a drop in the bucket of what is to come, I'm really looking forward to swimming in the ocean of it someday.

> Good gifts can become threats when we allow our affections for them to outgrow our desire for God Himself.

Until then, how are we to worship? Growing up, I always assumed that "worship" meant a Sunday morning or evening service in which one sings songs and hears a sermon. But it's so much more than that.

I love singing. It has been a passion of mine as far back as I can remember. God used *The Little Mermaid* to inspire me to start singing. (Go ahead and laugh.) It's a release for me. It's one of the ways I love to worship God. Not everyone loves singing. Some people hate it because it makes them uncomfortable, or they think that they can't carry a tune (and the "make a joyful *noise*" verse doesn't always encourage them). I remember friends who were constantly frustrated and beating themselves up for not enjoying singing praise and worship songs. They thought they were disappointing God. I wish I could have told them back then what I know now: "It's probably because God has given you a different way to worship Him!" Our usual definition of worship is far too limited.

So, what is worship? I would define worship as anything we do that makes us (and others) see God for who He is. We are worshiping God when we bring Him honor and glory out of our reverent devotion to Him.

What forms does worship come in? Here are a few of my ideas (and of course, there are many more).

- singing
- dancing
- painting
- looking at the stars
- sitting beside the ocean
- feeding the hungry
- taking soup to someone who's sick
- visiting a nursing home
- cooking a meal for neighbors
- taking a vow of silence
- studying church history
- discussing a deep theological truth
- taking communion
- tending a garden
- participating in a liturgy
- writing in a journal
- hugging people
- sitting quietly/meditation
- writing out what you believe
- letting someone go ahead of you in line
- being ethical at work and school
- tipping well when you go out to eat
- working to the best of your ability

Basically any and every action we take, word we say, or thought we think can be worshipful. We are making much of God when we live our lives sold out to loving Him and others. We are seeing God for who He is when we allow Him to transform our ways of thinking and when we let Him call the shots in our lives.

Why should I worship God? Forgive me if this seems too simplistic, but we should worship God because He is worthy. "When you think of what He has done for you, is this too much to ask?" (Rom. 12:1 NLT). The Psalmist wrote, "Ascribe to the LORD the glory due to His name; worship the LORD in holy array" (Ps. 29:2 NASB) and "Give honor to the LORD for the glory of his name. Worship the LORD in the splendor of his holiness" (NLT). Remember that we are in a covenant relationship with the King of the universe that goes both ways. As we look to Him in worship, we will find the deepest longings of our hearts fulfilled, even if it doesn't always look like we thought it would.

 As we look to Him in worship, we will find the deepest longings of our hearts fulfilled, even if it doesn't always look like we thought it would.

How should I worship God? This is where the fun part comes in for me. Whenever we would start a new season of community group, I would often have everyone take an awesome quiz/inventory that comes from the book *Sacred Pathways* by Gary Thomas.[3] It explores nine different "worship styles" (ways that people express their worship/relationship with God). I think the main point is not necessarily just to do activities that we enjoy, but instead to enjoy God through doing them.

Where should I worship God? I think that corporate, or group, worship is important. As I've mentioned, what form it takes is up to the group. I have friends who love to go hiking together. We have groups who make Christmas cards for those in nursing homes. We love putting together care kits for the homeless. We get together on Sundays and sing praises. We meet at coffee shops and pray. We gather in homes and study God's Word.

Worshiping God individually is equally important. We are each responsible for our own actions, thoughts, and words. We can utilize moments throughout our day to worship God. We are honoring Him each time we

- don't flip off the person who cut us off in traffic

- do our best at work or school, and not just when the boss/teacher is looking

- clean up after ourselves at a restaurant

- speak lovingly to our families

- engage in activities that flow with our worship styles

- seek His face in prayer, read His Word, and love others in practical ways

You'll recall our conversations about our being a royal priesthood. What does it mean to extend our identity as priests to worship? What kinds of sacrifices do we make? These verses come to mind for me:

> But the hour is coming, and is now here, when the true worshipers will worship the Father in spirit and truth, for the Father is seeking such people to worship him. God is spirit, and those who worship him must worship in spirit and truth. (John 4:23–24 ESV)

> Brothers and sisters, in light of *all I have shared with you about* God's mercies, I urge you to offer your bodies as a living and holy sacrifice *to God*, a sacred offering that brings Him pleasure; this is your reasonable, essential worship. (Rom. 12:1)

If our priestly duty is to offer sacrifices in worship, then our very lives are those sacrifices. We have been given the ministry of reconciliation—of calling the world to Jesus (2 Cor. 5:11–21). In light of all Jesus has done—indeed, He was the final sacrifice for sin—it is only reasonable that we in

turn give of ourselves. And when we give, we need to give the best we have to offer. These are sacrifices of worship rather than sacrifices of appeasement; remember, Jesus has already restored us to God. We can't earn more love or grace from God because we already have its endless supply. Instead we are to lay down our lives for one another. That is going to look different for each of us, but self-sacrifice will involve denying our own rights and desires, as it should. And although we may not always recognize it at the time, these sacrifices are what will bring us more fulfillment than we ever imagined. Let's give until it hurts, because it is for God's glory and for the good of others.

Stephen

Stephen's name comes from the Greek word *stephanos*, which means "crown." He was chosen along with six other men as the Church's first deacons. In the early church there were both Hebrews and Hellenists (Jews who lived within Greek language and culture), and though they held the same Jewish beliefs, they came from different backgrounds. There was quite a bit of tension between these groups, and an issue arose among them regarding the distribution of help for widows. The first deacons were tasked with tending the needy among them and ensuring that there was no favoritism in the dispersion of aid.

In light of all Jesus has done, it is only reasonable that we in turn give of ourselves.

Stephen was described as "full of faith and of the Holy Spirit" (Acts 6:5 ESV), "full of grace and power," and even as "doing great wonders and signs among the people" (Acts 6:8 ESV). He was noted for his wisdom and for speaking in the Spirit (Acts 6:10). His poignant speech recorded in Acts 7:2–53 reveals his grasp of Scripture, his faithfulness to Jesus as Messiah, his eloquence, and his bravery. Stephen communicated that God's salvation was intended for all people and was not reserved for Jews only.

The gospel was too much for the religious leaders, and they stirred up false witnesses to testify against Stephen, much the way they had against Jesus. Eventually the high council took Stephen outside the city and stoned him. As he was dying, Stephen echoed words that were fresh on his mind from another Man's execution: "Lord . . . receive my spirit. . . . Lord, do not hold this sin against them" (Acts 7:59–60 ESV). Stephen, a true worshiper, was the first Christian martyr.

Whether we are martyred or die of natural causes, may we all die with words of praise on our lips.

Even though he was faced with certain death, Stephen worshiped through his words and actions, giving of himself in the ultimate sacrifice. He saw Jesus standing at the right hand of God's throne, as though He was getting up to embrace Stephen as this inaugural martyr. Everywhere else in the New Testament, Jesus is described as seated at the throne. Imagine how powerful this vision must have been for Stephen, how reassuring and glorious.

As a result of Stephen's faithfulness and death, the majority of followers of the Way were forced to flee Jerusalem to escape widespread persecution. This led to the spread of the gospel in nations far and wide.

Are we so dedicated to Christ that we would die for His name's sake? How deep does our worship of God run? If we are in Christ and "full of faith and of the Holy Spirit," we very well may be called to follow in Stephen's footsteps. Whether we are martyred or die of natural causes, may we all die with words of praise on our lips.

Step into the Story

Romans 12:1–16

v. 1

BIG PICTURE:

Jesus was the final offering for sin, but our very lives should exist as offerings of worship. Check out Isaiah 1:16–20 and Micah 6:6–9.

¹ Brothers and sisters, in light of *all I have shared with you about* God's mercies, I urge you to offer your bodies as a living and holy sacrifice *to God*, a sacred offering that brings Him pleasure; this is your reasonable, essential worship. ² Do not allow this world to mold you in its own image. Instead, be transformed *from the inside out* by renewing your mind. As a result, you will be able to discern what God wills and whatever God finds good, pleasing, and complete.

v. 2

ORIGINAL AUDIENCE:

Check out the definition of the word *mind* (Strong's #G3563):

I. the mind, comprising alike the faculties of perceiving and understanding and those of feeling, judging, determining

  A. the intellectual faculty, the understanding

  B. reason in the narrower sense, as the capacity for spiritual truth, the higher powers of the soul, the faculty of perceiving divine things, of recognising goodness and of hating evil

  C. the power of considering and judging soberly, calmly and impartially

II. a particular mode of thinking and judging, i.e thoughts, feelings, purposes, desires[4]

³ Because of the grace allotted to me, I can *respectfully* tell you not to think of yourselves as being more important than you are; devote your minds to sound judgment since God has assigned to each of us a measure of faith. ⁴ For in the same way that one body has so many different parts, each with different functions; ⁵ we, too—the many—are different parts that form one body in the Anointed One. Each one of us is joined with one another, *and we become together what we could not be alone.* ⁶ Since our gifts vary depending on the grace poured out on each of us, *it is important that* we exercise the gifts *we have been given.* If prophecy is your gift, then speak as a prophet according to your proportion of faith. ⁷ If service is your gift, then serve well. If teaching is your gift, then teach well. ⁸ If you have been given a voice of encouragement, then use it *often.* If giving is your gift, then be generous. If leading, then be eager to get started. If sharing God's mercy, then be cheerful in sharing it.

⁹ Love others *well, and* don't hide behind a mask; love authentically. Despise evil; pursue what is good *as if your life depends on it.* ¹⁰ Live in true devotion to one another, loving each other as sisters and brothers. Be first to honor others *by putting them first.* ¹¹ Do not slack in your faithfulness and hard work. Let your spirit be on fire, bubbling up and boiling over, as you serve the Lord. ¹² *Do not forget to* rejoice, for hope is always just around the corner. Hold up through the hard times that are coming, and devote yourselves to prayer. ¹³ Share what you have with the saints, so they lack nothing; take every opportunity to open your *life and* home to others.

vv. 3–8

CONTEXT:

These verses could be seen as examples of what God finds good and pleasing and thus as outward results of a transformed mind. Worshiping through these avenues together is the fruit of being shaped into the likeness of Christ and not of the world.

v. 9–13

PRAYER:

Father, I so much want this to be the description of my life, lived as worship to You. Give me eyes to see the areas on which You want to work in me and the grace to cooperate with You as you rearrange me.

[14] If people mistreat or malign you, bless them. Always speak blessings, not curses. [15] If some have cause to celebrate, join in the celebration. And if others are weeping, join in that as well. [16] Work toward unity, and live in harmony with one another. Avoid thinking you are better than others or wiser than the rest; instead, embrace common people *and ordinary tasks*.

 **PRAYER**

 **BIG PICTURE**

 **CONTEXT**

 **ORIGINAL AUDIENCE**

 **STAND OUT MOMENTS**

Come Together

❖ How do you define *worship*?

❖ How do you define *success*?

❖ When was the last time you were truly happy? How does this tie to your fulfillment in Christ?

❖ In what area of your life is God asking for you to give till it hurts?

❖ Share a "Standout Moment" from this chapter and what you will do as a result.

> The chief end of man is to glorify God by enjoying Him forever.
>
> —John Piper[5]

Notes

CHAPTER TEN

VICTIM *avenged*

For we stand here, we.

If genuine artists, witnessing for God's

Complete, consummate, undivided work:

That not a natural flower can grow on earth,

Without a flower upon the spiritual side,

Substantial, archetypal, all a-glow

With blossoming causes, not so far away

—Elizabeth Barrett Browning (*Aurora Leigh*)[1]

In Christ, I am . . . avenged.

In Christ, you are . . . avenged.

Don't you know that He who pursues and explores the human heart *intimately* knows the Spirit's mind because He pleads to God for His saints to align their lives with the will of God? We are confident that God is able to orchestrate everything to work toward something

good *and beautiful* when we love Him and accept His invitation to live according to His plan. *From the distant past, His eternal love reached into the future.* You see, He knew those who would be His one day, and He chose them beforehand to be conformed to the image of His Son so that Jesus would be the firstborn of a new family of believers, all brothers and sisters. As for those He chose beforehand, He called them to a different destiny so that they would experience what it means to be made right with God and share in His glory.

So what should we say about all of this? If God is on our side, *then tell me*: whom should we fear? (Rom. 8:27–31)

The word *victim* conjures up various different emotions for people, doesn't it? Some of us have been told to stop playing the victim, implying that perhaps we are "blowing the whistle" for attention. But so very many of us, myself included, have truly been victimized. Statistics show that about one in four women were sexually abused[2], molested, or otherwise assaulted as children, and those are the conservative numbers. The statistics for domestic violence aren't any more encouraging. That means that, chances are, if you're a woman and you're reading this book, you very well may fall into the category of "victim." Or you probably know someone who does.

Injustice permeates our society, even if we haven't experienced it directly ourselves. It's enough to make anyone really angry, isn't it? Innocent children being victims of heinous crimes. Teen girls sold into slavery. Women beaten at the hands of their husbands, boyfriends, fathers. When we're in Christ, something within us gets a little bit riled up about those things, doesn't it? When we see injustice, a part of us wants to get up and do something about it.

How do you feel about the word *avenged*? My fellow comic book nerds will instantly think of the Avengers, but that's not where we're going with this. No, we're going beyond awesome storytelling and into the true gut of the Word. If anyone has the right to exact vengeance, it is the Creator of all things. If anyone in the universe has the right to be ticked enough to bring the bad guys to justice, it is the One True God.

Romans 12:17–21 has a good word for us on this topic. Even for those who may not identify with being a victim on the level we've described, you've probably been hurt by somebody. A friend has totally stabbed you in the back. Your boyfriend cheated on you. Your company laid you off. Your kid screamed in your face that he hates you. We've all got someone who has hurt us.

So what do we do about it? And what do we do when it feels as if God has just been standing by, letting these horrible things happen?

I'll never forget the day God spoke to me about this. My husband and I were driving down Briley Parkway, not far from where we lived in Nashville, talking about some pretty deep wounds in my life. Earlier that month I had begun therapy sessions to help deal with flashbacks I'd been having of childhood sexual abuse. The events of my childhood had been plaguing me my entire life, and I felt I had been robbed of so much over the years because of it. I started to see just how much those events had influenced my decisions and actions, and it made me so angry I couldn't stand it. So many questions were going through my mind—why didn't someone stop it? Why didn't someone do something once I had told them what happened? I got angrier and angrier and began to cry. Up until that point, I hadn't really allowed myself to be angry about what happened to me. The anger felt good. It felt justified. What had happened to me was wrong. It was evil. And I wanted someone to pay for it.

At that point I felt the gentlest words come to me, almost like an audible whisper: *"I did."*

> *What do we do when it feels as if God has just been standing by, letting these horrible things happen?*

I sat in silence as those words washed over me. It was as though Jesus were standing right in front of me, saying, "I feel your grief. I feel it stronger than you do. And I wanted someone to pay for it, too. So I did."

Up to that point I really had forgiven the perpetrators to the best of my ability. But something changed that day for me. Forgiveness went a little bit deeper than it ever had before. I accepted that Jesus had died for the perpetrators' sins.

I'm never going to get an apology from the people who molested me. Some of them I will never see again. Some of them may not think they did anything wrong. But I knew I had to forgive them anyway because otherwise the pain of their actions was going to eat me alive. Realizing Jesus had died for their sins, whether or not they ever sought my forgiveness—

It was as though Jesus were standing right in front of me, saying, "I feel your grief. I feel it stronger than you do. And I wanted someone to pay for it, too. So I did."

or His, for that matter—pushed that very forgiveness deep into my soul. If Jesus could die for my sin, He could die for theirs, too.

When we're in Christ, we've died to our own sin and walk in newness of life. We're new creations. We have been freed from sin. That means we can be free from other people's sin against us.

What it really boils down to is what we believe about God. Do we believe He cares? Do we believe He will make things right, whether we experience it directly or not?

Jesus taught nonviolence but cleansed the Temple violently—He is the only one who has the right to exercise judgment. He was avenging the people being cheated, but more important, avenging His glory.

Here's the bottom line about sin, and especially when the innocent are sinned against: it angers God more than it could ever anger us. All sin is ultimately against God. When God finally avenges His people and rights all wrongs, it isn't going to just be about restoring people and creation to what He originally intended; it is about ultimately revealing His glory. Every eye will see it, and everyone will acknowledge that He alone is God (Rom. 14:11).

★ ★ ★

Do not retaliate with evil, regardless of the evil brought against you. Try to do what is good *and right and honorable* as agreed upon by all people. If it is within your power, make peace with all people. *Again, my loved ones, do not seek revenge; instead, allow God's wrath to make sure justice is served. Turn it over to Him.* For the Scriptures say, "Revenge is Mine. I will settle all scores." But *consider this bit of wisdom:* "If your enemy is hungry, give him something to eat. If he is thirsty, give him something to drink; because if you treat him kindly, it will be like heaping hot coals on top of his head." Never let evil get the best of you; instead, overpower evil with the good. (Rom. 12:17–21)

Don't retaliate, regardless. Wow. That really hits me hard. Even with my own experience of forgiving the people who abused me. Because quite frankly, there are times when I just get plain mad. Someone hurts me, and I want to lash out and punish him or her for it. This is so far from the heart of God. Instead we are told, "Try to do what is good *and right and honorable*" (Rom. 12:17). "Make peace with all people" (v. 18). "Don't seek revenge" (v. 19). These phrases sometimes really rub up against my selfish desire for vindication. Maybe it's the same for you.

But check this out: the reason we aren't supposed to seek revenge is because we're supposed to let God do that. Yikes. So, if I am angry about what has happened to me personally and about all the injustice I see in the world, my anger is nothing compared to God's wrath. The idea of being on the receiving end of God's wrath strikes terror in my bones. It should strike terror in all of us. It may even strike so much terror in us that we feel a little bit sorry for those in His crosshairs. (Or it may not.) At any rate, to avoid getting in the way of God's execution of His wrath, we need to do good to those who hurt us. We watch for their needs and

help meet them. You may be thinking, *What? Are you kidding me?* This is so completely backward from what comes naturally to people, isn't it? It is something that we can do only through the power of the Holy Spirit.

Sometimes we see God's justice served. Sometimes we see the bad guys get caught and sent to jail. Sometimes we see the slaves freed. I love those moments. I have an inward surge of celebration every time I read a story about children rescued from the sex trade or about how the poor are being provided food and shelter. And I should. At the same time, I need to pray for those who are receiving judgment to see the error of their ways and turn to Christ. That's the really hard part. We don't have the luxury of hating our human enemies. We can hurl all the hatred we want at Satan. But as we've learned, people aren't our enemies. So we need to leave room for God to act by overcoming evil with good. This is the heart of forgiveness.

Does forgiving someone mean that we are condoning what he or she has done? No. While forgiving someone means we no longer hold bitterness and hatred against that person, it doesn't necessarily mean there are no longer consequences of what has occurred. Often, the natural consequences of sin are out of our control, but the power of that sin does not have to hold us in its grip. Does forgiving someone mean we must seek to restore or build a relationship with the one who has hurt us? Not always, but it might. There are some situations—those involving abuse, for example—when it may not be healthy for any of the parties involved to seek a close relationship with one another. But setting those exceptions aside, I do believe that it is wise to pursue reconciliation whenever possible. Imagine the hope and healing that can occur when we offer to one another the grace that God has shown us, or when we are shown it ourselves after wronging someone. Reconciliation between people is a beautiful picture of Christ's work on the cross and in our hearts.

I still struggle sometimes with all the evil I see in the world, especially when it seems as if nobody is doing anything to stop it. What do we do when it feels as though God is standing idly by while the world spins out of control? Let's take a look at the ancient Israelites.

God's people experienced about four hundred years of silence from Him during what is often called the *intertestamental period*. This is the span of time that passed between Malachi's last prophecy and Jesus' coming. Although there were no prophets during this time period, God was of course at work.[3] But take a look at some of the final words the people had heard from God:

> "For behold, the day is coming, burning like an oven, when all the arrogant and all evildoers will be stubble. The day that is coming shall set them ablaze, says the LORD of hosts, so that it will leave them neither root nor branch. But for you who fear my name, the sun of righteousness shall rise with healing in its wings. You shall go out leaping like calves from the stall. And you shall tread down the wicked, for they will be ashes under the soles of your feet, on the day when I act, says the LORD of hosts." (Mal. 4:1–3 ESV)

God promised His people that He would have the victory over evil and that He would make things right. I think it was probably difficult to hold on to that promise during those centuries of silence. To be honest, it is difficult even now to trust in that promise sometimes when I hear about the horrific details that happen everyday in this world. And then I come across scriptures like Psalm 9, and I'm reminded of God's faithfulness and closeness to us in our affliction:

> Still the Eternal remains and will reign forever;
>
> > He has taken His place on His throne for
> > judgment.
>
> So He will judge the world rightly.
>
> > He shall execute that judgment equally on all
> > people.

For the Eternal will be a shelter for those who
know misery,

a refuge during troubling times.

Those who know Your name will rely on You,

for You, O Eternal One, have not abandoned
those who search for You.

Praise Him who lives on Zion's holy hill.

Tell *the story* of His great acts among the
people!

For He remembers the victims of violence and
avenges their blood;

He does not turn a deaf ear to the cry of the
needy.

Be gracious to me, O Eternal One.

Notice the harm I have suffered because of
my enemies,

You who carry me safely away from death's
door,

So that I may rehearse Your deeds, declare Your
praise,

and rejoice in Your rescue

when I take my stand in the gates of Zion.

The nations have fallen into the pit they dug *for
others*,

their own feet caught, snared by the net they
hid.

The Eternal is *well* known, for He has taken
action and secured justice;

He has trapped the wicked through the work
of their own hands.

[pause with music]

The wicked are headed for death and the grave;

all the nations who forget the True God *will
share a similar fate.*

For those in need shall not always be forgotten,

and the hope of the poor will never die. (Ps.
9:7–18)

Ultimately, God wins. Christ is coming again and will avenge. We
have no need to fear. No matter what we experience on this earth, no matter how bad it gets, no matter how much affliction or persecution or pain
we might endure, God wins. No matter what "the end-times" look like,
no matter what the governments decide, no matter what religion prevails,
God wins. No matter what evil roams this earth. No matter what sicken-
ing things people do. No matter what, the Eternal remains and will reign
forever. And He will make things right.

When we are in Christ, we are safe. He's got this.

Joseph

When it comes to victimization, Joseph's experience could top most lists.
(You can check out his story in Genesis 37–50.) Joseph was the son of
Jacob (also called Israel) and Jacob's favorite wife, Rachel. He had one
younger brother, Benjamin, and Rachel died giving birth to him. Joseph
and Benjamin had ten other brothers, and every one of them despised
Joseph. See, when he was seventeen, Joseph had a dream that his brothers

were his servants, and he told them about this dream. This was probably not the smartest move in the world to make, but there you have it. Eventually Joseph's brothers got so tired of him that they threw him into a hole to die, but then later decided to sell him into slavery. Joseph ended up being sold to Potiphar, the captain of Pharaoh's guard in Egypt.

While he was in Egypt, Joseph did some maturing. The fact that the Lord was with him became undeniable, and he rose through the ranks in Potiphar's house. Everything was going well until Potiphar's wife tried to seduce Joseph. Being the godly man he was, he resisted. But the conniving woman found a way to falsely accuse him of rape, and Joseph ended up being arrested.

ften God calls us to go beyond the logical and bless those who have hurt us.

In prison, the Lord's presence with Joseph did not go unnoticed. Again Joseph was given responsibilities, and he faithfully performed his duties. He also gained a reputation for interpreting dreams, and after interpreting for Pharaoh's cupbearer, he hoped to finally have the record set straight about his innocence.

But the cupbearer forgot about Joseph, so he remained imprisoned for another two years. Can you imagine how Joseph must have felt through all of this? He was continually exploited even though he was faithful to the Lord.

Finally, Joseph caught a break. He was asked to interpret a particularly troubling dream for Pharaoh, and as a result ended up overseeing the food supply of Egypt and saved the nation from ruin during a seven-year, worldwide famine. At the age of thirty, Joseph was second only to Pharaoh. People heard about him far and wide, and neighboring nations sought him out for Egyptian aid.

Lo and behold, here came Joseph's brothers, in search of food for Israel. They had no clue that the man they were approaching was their long-lost brother. Joseph could have easily had them put to death or thrown in prison (the long interchange between him and his brothers in Genesis

42–44 is really interesting). But after dealing with his own personal turmoil, he wept and finally revealed himself to his family. What were his words to them?

> "Don't be upset or angry with yourselves *any longer* because of what you did. You see God sent me here ahead of you to preserve life. For famine struck this land two years ago, and there are five more years in which there will be no plowing or harvesting. God sent me *here* ahead of you to make sure you *and your families* survive *this terrible ordeal* and have a remnant left on earth. So it wasn't *really* you who sent me here, but God; the same God who made me an advisor to Pharaoh, master of his household, and ruler over everyone in the land of Egypt." (Gen. 45:5–8).

Much later, after Jacob had finally been reunited with his favorite son, he died. Joseph's brothers worried that with their father out of the picture, Joseph might decide to finally retaliate against them. But instead, Joseph's words were, "Don't be afraid. Am I *to judge* instead of God? *It is not my place.* Even though you intended to harm me, God intended it only for good, and through me, He preserved the lives of countless people, as He is still doing today. So don't worry. I will provide for you *myself*—for you and your children" (Gen. 50:19–21).

Joseph lived so much in God's presence that he was able to see the big picture of God's plan and not only forgive his perpetrators but bless them. There are definitely situations of abuse that do not warrant a restoration of relationship. But often God calls us to go beyond the logical and bless those who have hurt us.

> We know that all things work together for the good of those who love God: those who are called according to His purpose. (Romans 8:28 HCSB)

Step into the Story

Romans 12:17–21

vv. 19–20

BIG PICTURE:

Check out Deuteronomy 32:35 and Proverbs 25:21–22.

¹⁷ Do not retaliate with evil, regardless of the evil brought against you. Try to do what is good *and right and honorable* as agreed upon by all people. ¹⁸ If it is within your power, make peace with all people. ¹⁹ *Again,* my loved ones, do not seek revenge; instead, allow God's wrath *to make sure justice is served. Turn it over to Him.* For the Scriptures say, "Revenge is Mine. I will settle all scores." ²⁰ But *consider this bit of wisdom:* "If your enemy is hungry, give him something to eat. If he is thirsty, give him something to drink; because if you treat him kindly, it will be like heaping hot coals on top of his head." ²¹ Never let evil get the best of you; instead, overpower evil with the good.

v. 17

PRAYER:

Father, it is really tempting to lash out in anger at those who have hurt me. Please help me to step away from revenge and to pursue peace and kindness instead.

PRAYER

BIG PICTURE

CONTEXT

ORIGINAL AUDIENCE

STAND OUT MOMENTS

Come Together

❖ Is there a particular form of injustice that angers you a bit more than others? What is it?

❖ Is there anyone in your life to whom God wants you to extend His forgiveness?

❖ Have you ever experienced what felt like God's silence during a painful situation? How did you get through it?

❖ Share a "Standout Moment" from this chapter and what you will do as a result.

> *As for you, you meant evil against me, but God meant it for good, to bring it about that many people should be kept alive, as they are today.*
>
> **—Genesis 50:20 ESV**

Notes

CHAPTER ELEVEN

ROYALTY *Crowned*

All that is gold does not glitter,

Not all those who wander are lost;

The old that is strong does not wither,

Deep roots are not reached by the frost.

From the ashes a fire shall be woken,

A light from the shadows shall spring;

Renewed shall be blade that was broken,

The crownless again shall be king.

—J. R. R. Tolkien, *The Fellowship of the Ring* [1]

In Christ, I am . . . an heir.

In Christ, you are . . . an heir.

If we are God's children, that means we are His heirs along with the Anointed, set to inherit everything that is His. If we share His sufferings, *we know that* we will ultimately share in His glory.

Now I'm sure of this: the sufferings we endure now are not even worth comparing to the glory that is coming and will be revealed in us. For all of creation is waiting, yearning for the time when the children of God will be revealed. You see, all of creation has collapsed into emptiness, not by its own choosing, but by God's. Still He placed within it a *deep and abiding* hope that creation would one day be liberated from its slavery to corruption and experience the glorious freedom of the children of God. For we know that all creation groans *in unison* with birthing pains up until now. *And there is more;* it's not just creation—all of us are groaning together too. Though we have already tasted the firstfruits of the Spirit, we are longing for the total redemption of our bodies that comes when our adoption as children *of God* is complete— for we have been saved in this hope *and for this future*. But hope does not involve what we already *have or* see. For who goes around hoping for what he already has? But if we wait expectantly for things we have never seen, then we hope with true perseverance and eager anticipation. (Rom. 8:17–25)

It's rare for the majority of people in American culture to personally experience what it means to have an inheritance. Most of us don't come from wealthy families that have estates passed down from generation to generation. We may have family heirlooms, and some of those items could hold financial value as well as sentimental value. Many of us may have families with life insurance policies or some other arrangement that distributes money or other possessions upon a person's death. But most of us don't live in the reality of the rich and famous and aren't waiting to inherit millions of dollars and a beach house.

There are lots of complex laws on the books in the United States about inheritances and all the taxes that go along with them, and people are free to leave their property to whomever they want. This process is similar to the New Testament world, though in general, a family's wealth was passed on to the father's sons, with the eldest son receiving a double portion. However, religion professors Hanson and Oakman note:

Inheritance is the means of distributing the family's movable and immovable property after the death of the patriarch. It transfers the property from one generation to the next, providing the sustenance of the family, the possession of the land, and acknowledgment of patron-client obligations. The aspects often overlooked by historians have been the function of dowries as premortem inheritance, the return of the wife's dowry and indirect dowry, the contingencies of inheritance distribution, and the acknowledgment of patron/client relationships.[2]

Hanson and Oakman point out that the estate of Herod the Great was distributed among several family members and patrons, including women, and not exclusively to his sons.

This historical context is interesting to me and brings many questions to mind as I read through the portions of the New Testament that mention our inheritance in Christ. Now, our inheritance doesn't work according to earthly laws (God isn't going to someday magically die, for instance)—Jesus as God in the flesh has already died and come back to life. As God's only Son, Jesus inherits everything in the universe, right? So what does it mean that we also are heirs with Christ (Rom. 8:17)? Which parts of the inheritance do we already have, and are there any parts we have to wait to access until we ourselves have entered heaven?

> Since you belong to Him *and are now subject to His power*, you are the descendant of Abraham and the heir *of God's glory* according to the promise.
>
> Listen. I am going to explain *how this all works*: When a minor inherits an estate *from his parents*, although he is the owner of everything, he is the same as a slave. Until the day set by his father, the minor is subject to the authorities or guardians *whom his father put in charge*. It is like that with us; there was a time when we were like children held under the elemental powers of this world. When the right time arrived, God sent His Son into this world (born of a woman, subject to the law) to free those who, *just like Him*, were subject to the law. Ultimately He wanted us all to be adopted as sons and daughters. Because you are now part of God's family, He sent the Spirit of His Son into our hearts; *and*

the Spirit calls out, "Abba, Father." You no longer have to live as a slave because you are a child *of God*. And since you are His child, God guarantees an inheritance *is waiting* for you. (Gal. 3:29—4:7)

Galatians 3:29 notes that we have access to Abraham's inheritance since we are connected to him through faith. What was Abraham's inheritance? In Hebrews 11 we read, "By faith Abraham heard God's call to travel to a place he would one day receive as an inheritance; and he obeyed, not knowing where God's call would take him. By faith he journeyed to the land of the promise as a foreigner; he lived in tents, as did Isaac and Jacob, his fellow heirs to the promise because Abraham looked ahead to a city with foundations, a city laid out and built by God" (vv. 8–10). God had promised Abraham more descendants than anyone could count (Gen.15:5) and a large, fertile land (Gen. 15:18–21). I think we're all aware of the constant battle over the land of Israel/Palestine. People much smarter than I am have written volumes on this, and we just don't have the capacity to discuss it here. I think we can be assured that God's kingdom is here and now, isn't limited to political or geographical borders, and is open to all who trust in Christ. Moreover, His kingdom isn't bound by time or space. While we can reap its benefits here and now, it is a mere shadow of what we will experience on the other side of eternity.

> *You* no longer have to live as a slave because you are a child *of God*. And since you are His child, God guarantees an inheritance *is waiting* for you.

So, are all Christians able to benefit from Abraham's inheritance? From what he wrote in Ephesians 3:6, Paul certainly thought so. "Specifically, *the mystery* is this: by trusting in the good news, the Gentile outsiders are becoming *fully enfranchised* members of the same body, heirs alongside *Israel,* and beneficiaries of the promise *that has been fulfilled* through Jesus the Anointed." Apparently our

inheritance is not just individually based, although there are implications for each of us individually. Our inheritance is a family priority. It is meant to be experienced in community. Check out other translations of this verse; "fellow heir" is often used. Our inheritance in Christ is experienced with others.

Hebrews 11:39–40 definitely reveals this as the heart of God. In this eleventh chapter of Hebrews (known to those of us who grew up in Sunday school as the Hall of Faith), the writer recounted all that our spiritual ancestors did because they trusted God. But throughout, the writer was trying to help us see that even though our ancestors faithfully followed God, they didn't receive the fullness of the promise. Not until Jesus' redemptive act did the promise become fully realized: "These, though commended by God for their great faith, did not receive what was promised. That promise has awaited us, who receive the better thing that God has provided *in these last days*, so that with us, our forebears might finally see the promise completed" (vv. 39–40).

So the next time I feel that the things God has called me to do are mundane, annoying, or uncomfortable, I need to remember that Sarah and Abraham and Rahab are finally experiencing what they couldn't here on earth because I am experiencing the fullness of God's promises to them. "So since we stand surrounded by *all those who have gone before,* an enormous cloud of witnesses, let us drop every extra weight, every sin that clings to us *and slackens our pace,* and let us run with endurance the long race set before us" (Heb.12:1). This needs to change the way we live our lives. Not only are we a part of the current Body of Christ as it stands on earth in this moment; we are connected to an unfathomable network of His children across time and space.

"If we are God's children, that means we are His heirs along with the Anointed, set to inherit everything that is His. If we share His sufferings, *we know that* we will ultimately share in His glory" (Rom. 8:17). On this side of eternity we will experience suffering. But suffering isn't the end for us. "No, in all these things we are more than conquerors through him who

loved us" (Rom. 8:37 ESV). "He brought us *out of our old ways of living* to a new beginning through the washing of regeneration; and He made us completely new through the Holy Spirit, who was poured out in abundance through Jesus the Anointed, our Savior. *All of this happened* so that through His grace we would be accepted *into God's covenant family* and appointed to be His heirs, full of the hope that comes from *knowing you have* eternal life" (Titus 3:5-7). When I read this passage, peace settles over me; the whole reason Jesus redeemed us, the whole reason God has done everything He has, the whole reason He has blessed us, the whole reason He has allowed the "bad things" to happen is so that He would be glorified by our becoming a part of His family and our inheriting what He has in store for us.

Beyond the majesty we can see with our eyes, our beautiful inheritance in Christ is best viewed with the heart.

What does this inheritance look like here and now? What comes to mind for you when you think of the untold riches of the kingdom of God? Could some of it be physical? When I hear the ocean waves or stare up at a colossal mountain, I know God's kingdom is beautiful. And yet, "all of creation is waiting, yearning for the time when the children of God will be revealed. You see, all of creation has collapsed into emptiness, not by its own choosing, but by God's. Still He placed within it a *deep and abiding* hope that creation would one day be liberated from its slavery to corruption and experience the glorious freedom of the children of God" (Rom. 8:19–21). If we think what we see now is amazing, we know that it is going to be even more incredible someday. But beyond the majesty we can see with our eyes, our beautiful inheritance in Christ is best viewed with the heart. We hope in riches we haven't seen yet, although they are things we have tastes of here and now. I think of love, joy, peace, patience, kindness, goodness, faithfulness, gentleness, self-control, freedom from fear, and the ability to forgive. These are qualities the indwelling Spirit produces within us as we allow Him to continually shape us into the likeness of Christ, and these are treasures that can never be destroyed.

Our inheritance is eternal. Since God decides who receives His riches, there isn't anything we can do to earn them. Likewise, there isn't anything we can do that would make Him revoke them. In Christ, we've been sealed with the Holy Spirit and adopted as children into His family. God is never going to turn His back on Jesus, and therefore He will never turn on us.

> He has enlightened us to the great mystery *at the center* of His will. With immense pleasure, He laid out His intentions *through Jesus*, a plan that will climax when the time is right *as He returns to create order and unity*— both in heaven and on earth—when all things are brought together under the Anointed's *royal rule*. In Him we stand to inherit even more. As His heirs, we are predestined *to play a key role* in His *unfolding* purpose that is energizing everything to conform to His will. As a result, we—the first to place our hope in the Anointed One—will live in a way to bring Him glory and praise. Because you, too, have heard the word of truth—the good news of your salvation—and because you believed *in the One who is truth*, your lives are marked with His seal. This is *none other than* the Holy Spirit who was promised as the guarantee toward the inheritance we are to receive when He frees and rescues all who belong to Him. To God be all praise and glory! . . . Open the eyes of their hearts, *and let the light of Your truth flood in*. Shine Your light on the hope You are calling them to embrace. Reveal to them the glorious riches You are preparing as their inheritance. (Eph. 1:9–14, 18)

> Thank You, Father, as You have made us eligible to receive our portion of the inheritance given to all those set apart by the light. You have rescued us from dark powers and brought us safely into the kingdom of Your Son, whom You love and in whom we are redeemed and forgiven of our sins [through His blood]. (Col. 1:12–14)

Everyone who is in Christ—set apart by the light—is a part of the kingdom and has a portion in this inheritance. The defining characteristic is the Holy Spirit. What does it mean to be marked with His seal?

Seal: to set a seal upon, mark with a seal, to seal

1. for security: from Satan

2. since things sealed up are concealed (as the contents of a letter), to hide, keep in silence, keep secret

3. in order to mark a person or a thing

    1. to set a mark upon by the impress of a seal or a stamp

    2. angels are said to be sealed by God

4. in order to prove, confirm, or attest a thing
5. to confirm authenticate, place beyond doubt

    1. of a written document

    2. to prove one's testimony to a person that he is what he professes to be[3]

The Holy Spirit keeps us safe from Satan; while the enemy may disrupt our lives, he can never touch our souls. Nothing can separate us from God. The Holy Spirit marks us as His; He is the proof that we are who we are, that we are in Christ, and He proves our identity as we become more like Christ.

I grew up not really understanding who the Holy Spirit is. In fact, I grew up with some really wacky ideas about Him. For starters, I thought of Him as an "it." "It" was really mysterious and probably even a little scary. The people in church sometimes even called "it" a ghost—a holy one, but still, a ghost. I had watched enough *Unsolved Mysteries* to be a little freaked out by that word. Also, I would sometimes hear that through the power of the Holy Spirit, people were able to do really miraculous deeds. That sounded cool to me. But up until my college years, I really didn't think too much about the Holy Spirit. I knew He/it was part of the Trinity, and that was important, but I didn't take much time to discover why.

Then in college I made friends with some students who were from a much different background than mine. They stressed the importance of the Holy Spirit and the gifts He gives. I was very intrigued by this new and interesting aspect of God. These folks could pray in other languages and all kinds of cool stuff. I even witnessed a bona fide physical healing after a friend and I prayed quietly for a girl with an almost-broken ankle (she was able to walk on it immediately after having had to use crutches). I thought for sure I had leveled up in my relationship with God somehow after that.

Over the years following college, I did a lot of reading and studying and came to a balanced understanding of the role of the Holy Spirit in my life and what I believe His role is for all who are in Christ. For those of us in Christ, the Holy Spirit is the very life within us. If you're in Christ, take a moment to just completely let this hit you. The power of God resides within you. Not just His power. Him. His nature, His very being. The God who spoke the universe into existence dwells in you. The God who raises the dead lives in you. Is this not the biggest deal ever? I mean, wow. When we really grasp the fact that the one true God has chosen to make His home in us, that has got to change things. It has to change everything—the way we think, the way we feel, the way we view ourselves and others. It should enable us to be content in all circumstances

> *For those of us in Christ, the Holy Spirit is the very life within us.*

(Phil. 4:13), increasingly make us more like Him (Gal. 5:19–23), and give us victory over sin as we submit to His leadership (2 Cor. 10:3–6). It also changes the way we view our future. As children of the King, we are royalty who will one day enjoy eternity in the presence of God, casting our crowns at His feet.

Although we are royalty, we are to live humbly and with constant awareness of those around us—we must set aside our selfish ambitions and seek out those who have yet to worship God.

When the Son of Man comes in all His majesty accompanied by throngs of heavenly messengers, His throne will be wondrous. All the nations will assemble before Him, and He will judge them, distinguishing them from one another as a shepherd isolates the sheep from the goats. He will put some, the sheep, at His right hand and some, the goats, at His left. Then the King will say to those to His right,

King: Come here, *you beloved*, you people whom My Father has blessed. Claim your inheritance, the Kingdom prepared for you from the beginning of creation. *You shall be richly rewarded*, for when I was hungry, you fed Me. And when I was thirsty, you gave Me something to drink. I was alone as a stranger, and you welcomed Me *into your homes and into your lives*. I was naked, and you gave Me clothes to wear; I was sick, and you tended to My needs; I was in prison, and you comforted Me.

Even then the righteous *will not have achieved perfect understanding and will not recall these things*.

Righteous: Master, when did we find You hungry and give You food? When did we find You thirsty and slake Your thirst? When did we find You a stranger and welcome You in, or find You naked and clothe You? When did we find You sick *and nurse You to health*? When did we visit You when You were in prison?

King: I tell you this: whenever you saw a brother *or sister hungry or cold*, whatever you did to the least of these, so you did to Me. (Matt. 25:31–40)

If we're sealed with the Spirit and He is our defining characteristic, eventually His love will pour out of us so naturally that we don't remember the righteous things we've done as being anything out of the ordinary. Oh, that in our lifetimes we would be intentional enough to seek out the prisoners and unoccupied enough to notice the people in need around us!

When Christ comes again, He will bring everything full circle. Gone will be the corrupt world system and sin that ruined humanity from the beginning. The kingdom will be completed here on earth just as it is in heaven. We will have a role to play as God's will is acted out, and it will glorify Him. We will without a doubt receive the fullness of our inheritance. What does it mean to share in His glory? Could it be that His people become His crowning glory (see Isaiah 62:3; Zechariah 9:16)? Everything will be set right—even better than it was in the garden of Eden. His people will be restored to fully glorify God in ways never seen or imagined. As we pursue humility and worship of the one true God, losing ourselves in Him and giving our lives away for His name's sake, He will be glorified here and now. And one day, everything humanity has experienced will have merely been the beginning of the story:

> No one or nothing will labor under any curse any longer. And the throne of God and of the Lamb will sit *prominently* in the city. God's servants will *continually* serve *and worship* Him. They will be able to look upon His face, and His name will be written on their foreheads. Darkness will never again fall *on this city*. They will not require the light of a lamp or of the sun because the Lord God will be their illumination. *By His light*, they will reign throughout the ages. (Rev. 22:3–5)

> I will not keep quiet for Zion's sake;
>
> > I will not remain silent
>
> Until Jerusalem's justice shines like the light of a
> > new day
>
> > and her liberation blazes like a torch *in the*
> > > *dead of night.*
>
> *Jerusalem*, the nations *of the world* will witness
> > your righteousness,
>
> > the most powerful world leaders will see your
> > > brilliance,
>
> And you will be called something new, *something*
> > *brand new,*
>
> > a name given by *none other than* the Eternal
> > > One.

And you will be the crowning glory of the
    Eternal's *power*,

> a royal crown cradled in His palm and held
>   aloft by your God *for all to see.*

People won't talk about you anymore

> using words like "forsaken" or "empty."

Instead, you will be called "My delight" and the
    land around you "Married,"

> because the Eternal is pleased with you and
>   has bound Himself to your land.

As a young man marries the woman *he loves*,

> so your sons will marry you, Jerusalem.

As a groom takes joy in his bride,

> so your God will take joy in you. (Isa.
>   62:1–5)

In the end, God will reign as our King and we will be His in ways previously unimaginable. God is the One and Only true King. We are His people, His beloved children. May we live like we know it.

> On that day the LORD their God will rescue his
>   people,

>> just as a shepherd rescues his sheep.

> They will sparkle in his land

>> like jewels in a crown.

> How wonderful and beautiful they will be!

> The young men will thrive on abundant
> grain,
>
> and the young women will flourish on new
> wine. (Zech. 9:16–17 NLT)

David

David was anointed as king of Israel at age fifteen, but it took twenty-two years for him to actually sit on the throne. The day after he was anointed, he went back to tending the sheep. Later he was promoted to taking lunch to his brothers. All along he was still the anointed king.

I imagine that David was probably tempted to doubt his anointing at some point—perhaps even several points. After all, not only was he not king, but the current king, Saul, was determined to kill him. But David held onto the promise that he was God's choice to lead Israel, even if he wasn't doing it just yet.

David didn't just merely survive for those twenty-two years; he thrived. He didn't sit around moping about his circumstances. He took down Goliath, became a skilled warrior, and nurtured a heart that beat for God. He utilized his time of waiting very well. Keeping his eyes on God and believing His promises, David became more and more of the king God had already called him to be, even though he didn't have the title yet. He lived his life in pursuit of God, knowing that each day existed not only for the present moment but for the future of an entire nation.

We are in Christ. His Spirit dwells within us. Our destinies are secure. We have everything we need to thrive each day, to God's glory. So, like David, during our time of waiting, may we become more of who we really are.

Step into the Story

What do you think? Are you ready to take a crack at this one totally on your own? I'm grinning from ear to ear, praying for you, and cheering you on!

*R*omans 4

¹ In light of all of this, what should we say about our ancestor Abraham? ² If Abraham was made right by performing certain works, then he would surely have something to brag about. Right? Not before *the Creator* God, ³ because as the Scriptures say, "Abraham believed God *and trusted in His promises,* so God counted it to his favor as righteousness." ⁴ Now, when you work a job, do your wages come as a gift *or as compensation for your work*? It is *most certainly* not a gift—you are only paid what you have earned. ⁵ So for the person who does not work, but instead trusts in the One who makes the ungodly right, his faith is counted for him as righteousness.

⁶ *Remember the psalm where* David speaks about the benefits that come to the person whom God credits with righteousness apart from works? He said,

⁷ Blessed are those whose wrongs have been forgiven

and whose sins have been covered.

⁸ Blessed is the person whose sin the Lord will not take into account.

⁹ So is this blessing spoken only for the circumcised or for all uncircumcised people too? We remind *you what the Scripture has to say*: faith was credited to Abraham as righteousness.

¹⁰ So when was the credit awarded *to Abraham*? Was it before or after his circumcision? Well, it certainly wasn't after—it was before he was circumcised. ¹¹ *Eventually* he was given circumcision as a sign of his right standing, indicating that he was credited on the basis of the faith he possessed before he was circumcised. It happened this way so that Abraham might become the spiritual father of all those who are not circumcised but are made right through their faith. ¹² In the same

way, *God destined him to be* the spiritual father of all those who are cir-cumcised as more than an outward sign, but who walk in our father Abraham's faithful footsteps—a faith he possessed while he was still uncircumcised.

¹³ The promise given to Abraham and his children, that one day they would inherit the world, did not come because he followed the rules of the law. It came as a result of his right standing *before God, a standing he* obtained through faith. ¹⁴ If this inheritance is available only to those who keep the law, then faith is a useless commodity and the promise is canceled. ¹⁵ For the law brings God's wrath *against sin*. But where the law doesn't draw the line, there can be no crime.

¹⁶ This is the reason that faith is the single source of the promise—so that grace would be offered to all Abraham's children, those whose lives are defined by the law and those who follow the path of faith charted by Abraham, our common father. ¹⁷ As it is recorded *in the Scriptures*, "I have appointed you the father of many nations." In the presence of the God who creates out of nothing and holds the power to bring to life what is dead, Abraham believed *and so became our father*.

> braham believed God *and trusted in His promises*, so God counted it to his favor as righteousness.
> (Rom. 4:4)

¹⁸ Against the odds, Abraham's hope grew into full-fledged faith that he would turn out to be the father of many nations, just as God had promised when He said, "That's how *many* your descendants will be." ¹⁹ His faith did not fail, although he was well aware that his impotent body, after nearly 100 years, was as good as dead and that Sarah's womb, too, was dead. ²⁰ In spite of all this, his faith in God's promise did not falter. In fact, his faith grew as he gave glory to God ²¹ because he was supremely confident that God could deliver on His promise. ²² This is why, *you see, God saw* his faith *and* counted him as righteous; *this is how he became* right with God.

²³ The story of how faith was credited to Abraham was not recorded for him and him alone, ²⁴ but was written for all of us who would one day be credited for having faith in God, the One who raised Jesus our

Lord from the realm of the dead. [25] He was delivered over to death for our trespasses and raised so that we might be made right *with God*.

Come Together

❖ Do you view yourself as a child of royalty? How might that affect your daily life?

❖ What do you imagine it will be like to experience all of creation restored to the glory God intended?

❖ What are some of the riches of Christ that you need to experience in your life right now?

❖ If the forerunners of our faith are cheering us on as we live life in Christ, how does that change the way you view the situations you find yourself in today?

❖ Share a "Standout Moment" from this chapter and what you will do as a result.

And for us this is the end of all the stories, and we can most truly say that they all lived happily ever after. But for them it was only the beginning of the real story. All their life in this world . . . had only been the cover and the title page: now at last they were beginning Chapter One of the Great Story which no one on earth has read: which goes on forever: in which every chapter is better than the one before.

—C. S. Lewis, *The Last Battle* [5]

Notes

Acknowledgments

I need to thank:

Leonard Sweet, for your unwavering support and encouragement.

Gary Morgan and Pete Williamson, for your pastoral guidance, solid preaching, and prayers.

My Mosaic (Nashville, TN) and Oikos Fellowship (Bellingham, WA) church families, especially our small groups. Thank you for being the church.

GB Howell, Nicole Taher, Kat DeVaney, and my mom, Anne Atkins, for your assistance in research and your invaluable manuscript feedback.

My fellow InScribed collection authors: Wendy Blight, Donna Gaines, Amanda Hope Haley, Jenifer Jernigan, Sarah Francis Martin, and Heather Zempel. I'm honored to call you friends.

The InScribed team at Thomas Nelson: Frank Couch, Maleah Bell, Alee Anderson, Jennifer Keller, Bethany Carlson, Blythe Daniel, Kate Mulvaney, Robin Crosslin, Lisa Lester, Jerri Helms, Jaime Guthals, the entire sales team, and countless others who have believed in us.

Beth Moore, although I haven't met her. I feel as though I stand on the "shoulders" of her *Believing God* study and the truths within it.

Allison Duke, for being my best friend since first grade and for laboring through this book with me. It wouldn't have happened without you!

Xavier, my little man—I want you to know that I tried to write this book while you were sleeping. I will always choose you over work.

Aaron, the love of my life, you've been beside me every step of this journey. I would not be who I am without you.

And last but certainly not least, my prayer warriors. I am so richly blessed with you there isn't enough room to list you all here. Thank you for interceding for me and loving me!

Appendix 1

For Further Reading

Jesus: A Theography by Leonard Sweet and Frank Viola (Nashville: Thomas Nelson, 2012)

Made Right

Gospel: Recovering the Power that Made Christianity Revolutionary by J. D. Greear and Timothy Keller (Nashville: B&H, 2013)

The Jesus Storybook Bible: Every Story Whispers His Name by Sally Lloyd-Jones (Grand Rapids: ZonderKidz, 2012)

The Ragamuffin Gospel: Good News for the Bedraggled, Beat-Up, and Burnt Out by Brennan Manning (Colorado Springs: Multnomah, 2008)

Corpse Alive

The Divine Conspiracy: Rediscovering Our Hidden Life in God by Dallas Willard (HarperSanFrancisco, 2008)

The Passion of Jesus Christ: Fifty Reasons Why He Came to Die by John Piper (Wheaton, IL: Crossway, 2004)

Forgotten God: Reversing Our Tragic Neglect of the Holy Spirit by Francis Chan (Colorado Springs: David C. Cook, 2009)

Failure Commissioned

Compelled by Love: The Most Excellent Way to Missional Living by Ed Stetzer and Philip Nation (n.p.: New Hope Publishers, 2008)

The Hole in Our Gospel: What Does God Expect of Us? The Answer That Changed My Life and Might Just Change the World by Richard Stearns (Nashville: Thomas Nelson, 2009)

A Work of Heart: Understanding How God Shapes Spiritual Leaders by Reggie McNeal (New York: Jossey-Bass, 2011)

Appendix 1 (Continued)

Saint

Battlefield of the Mind: Winning the Battle in Your Mind by Joyce Meyer (Tulsa: Harrison House, 1995)

Outlaw by Ted Dekker (n.p.: Center Street, 2013)

The Screwtape Letters by C. S. Lewis (New York: Time Inc., 1961)

Peacemaker

Fight: A Christian Case for Nonviolence by Preston Sprinkle (Colorado Springs: David C. Cook, 2013)

Nonviolent Communication: A Language of Life by Marshall Rosenberg (n.p.: San Val, 2003)

Tea with Hezbollah: Sitting at the Enemies' Table by Ted Dekker and Carl Medearis (New York: Doubleday Religion, 2010)

Sister

Center Church: Doing Balanced, Gospel-Centered Ministry in Your City by Timothy J. Keller (Grand Rapids: Zondervan, 2012)

Incarnate: The Body of Christ in an Age of Disengagement by Michael Frost (Downers Grove, IL: InterVarsity, 2014)

Life Together by Dietrich Bonhoeffer (New York: Harper & Row, 1954)

Messy Spirituality by Mike Yaconelli (Grand Rapids: Zondervan, 2009)

Dwelling Occupied

Mere Discipleship: Radical Christianity in a Rebellious World by Lee Camp (Grand Rapids: Brazos, 2008)

A Woman's Heart: God's Dwelling Place by Beth Moore (Nashville: LifeWay, 2007)

Worshiper Fulfilled

Desiring God: Meditations of a Christian Hedonist by John Piper (Colorado Springs: Multnomah, 2011)

Gods at War: Defeating the Idols that Battle for Your Heart by Kyle Idleman (Grand Rapids: Zondervan, 2012)

Sacred Pathways: Discover Your Soul's Path by Gary Thomas (Nashville: Thomas Nelson, 1996)

Victim Avenged

Rid of My Disgrace: Hope and Healing for Victims of Sexual Assault by Justin and Lindsey Holcomb (Wheaton, IL: Crossway, 2011)

The Search for Significance: Seeing Your True Worth Through God's Eyes by Robert S. McGee (Nashville: Thomas Nelson, 2003)

Royalty Crowned

Safely Home by Randy Alcorn (Grand Rapids: Tyndale, 2001)

Appendix 2

In Christ, I am . . .

This is a list that I've compiled over the years. Feel free to add more verses as you find them in your Bible reading in the future.

In Christ, I am . . .

❀ Chosen

❀ Formed by God

❀ Set apart

❀ Appointed to the nations

❀ Sent

(Jeremiah 1:4–5)

❀ Blessed

❀ Chosen

❀ Holy

❀ Blameless

❀ Loved

❀ Adopted

❀ Favored

❖ Redeemed

❖ Forgiven

❖ His inheritance

❖ Sealed with the Spirit

(Ephesians 1:3–14)

❖ Not disappointed

❖ A living stone

❖ Part of a chosen race

❖ Part of a royal priesthood

❖ Part of a holy nation

❖ God's possession

(1 Peter 2:5–10)

❖ Dead to sin

❖ Alive to God

Romans 6:11)

Appendix 2 (Continued)

❖ Not condemned

(Romans 8:1)

❖ An important member of the body

Romans 12:5)

❖ Washed

❖ Sanctified

❖ Justified

(1 Corinthians 6:11)

❖ Led in triumph

❖ The fragrance of Christ

(2 Corinthians 2:14–15)

❖ Unveiled

(2 Corinthians 3:14)

❖ A new creation

❖ Reconciled

❖ A minister of reconciliation

(2 Corinthians 5:17–19)

❖ Crucified with Christ

❖ Alive in Christ by faith

❖ Loved

(Galatians 2:20)

❖ God's daughter

(Galatians 3:26)

❖ Loved

❖ Made alive

❖ Raised up and seated with Him

❖ His workmanship

❖ Created for good works

Appendix 2 (Continued)

❖ Brought near to God

(Ephesians 2:4–10, 13)

❖ An heir and member of the body

❖ A partaker of the promise

(Ephesians 3:6)

❖ Righteous

(Philippians 3:9)

❖ Cared for by God

(1 Peter 5:7)

❖ Restored

❖ Confirmed

❖ Strengthened

❖ Established

(1 Peter 5:10)

Notes

Appendix 3

Romans Reading Plan

*D*ay 1: Romans 1:1–15

*D*ay 2: Romans 1:16–3:20

*D*ay 3: Romans 3:21–5:21

*D*ay 4: Romans 6:1–8:39

*D*ay 5: Romans 9:1–11:36

*D*ay 6: Romans 12:1–15:13

*D*ay 7: Romans 15:14–16:27

Appendix 4

READ YOUR BIBLE THROUGH IN A YEAR

A systematic division of the books of the Bible, primarily for reading.

JANUARY

DATE	MORNING	EVENING
	MATT.	GEN.
1	1	1, 2, 3
2	2	4, 5, 6
3	3	7, 8, 9
4	4	10, 11, 12
5	5: 1-26	13, 14, 15
6	5:27-48	16, 17
7	6: 1-18	18, 19
8	6:19-34	20, 21, 22
9	7	23, 24
10	8: 1-17	25, 26
11	8:18-34	27, 28
12	9: 1-17	29, 30
13	9:18-38	31, 32
14	10: 1-20	33, 34, 35
15	10:21-42	36, 37, 38
16	11	39, 40
17	12: 1-23	41, 42
18	12:24-50	43, 44, 45
19	13: 1-30	46, 47, 48
20	13:31-58	49, 50
		EX.
21	14: 1-21	1, 2, 3
22	14:22-36	4, 5, 6
23	15: 1-20	7, 8
24	15:21-39	9, 10, 11
25	16	12, 13
26	17	14, 15
27	18: 1-20	16, 17, 18
28	18:21-35	19, 20
29	19	21, 22
30	20: 1-16	23, 24
31	20:17-34	25, 26

FEBRUARY

DATE	MORNING	EVENING
	MATT.	EX.
1	21: 1-22	27, 28
2	21:23-46	29, 30
3	22: 1-22	31, 32, 33
4	22:23-46	34, 35
5	23: 1-22	36, 37, 38
6	23:23-39	39, 40
		LEV.
7	24: 1-28	1, 2, 3
8	24:29-51	4, 5
9	25: 1-30	6, 7
10	25:31-46	8, 9, 10
11	26: 1-25	11, 12
12	26:26-50	13
13	26:51-75	14
14	27: 1-26	15, 16
15	27:27-50	17, 18
16	27:51-66	19, 20
17	28	21, 22
	MARK	
18	1: 1-22	23, 24
19	1:23-45	25
20	2	26, 27
		NUM.
21	3: 1-19	1, 2
22	3:20-35	3, 4
23	4: 1-20	5, 6
24	4:21-41	7, 8
25	5: 1-20	9, 10, 11
26	5:21-43	12, 13, 14
27	6: 1-29	15, 16
28	6:30-56	17, 18, 19
29	7: 1-13	20, 21, 22

MARCH

DATE	MORNING	EVENING
	MARK	NUM.
1	7:14-37	23, 24, 25
2	8: 1-21	26, 27
3	8:22-38	28, 29, 30
4	9: 1-29	31, 32, 33
5	9:30-50	34, 35, 36
		DEUT.
6	10: 1-31	1, 2
7	10:32-52	3, 4
8	11: 1-18	5, 6, 7
9	11:19-33	8, 9, 10
10	12: 1-27	11, 12, 13
11	12:28-44	14, 15, 16
12	13: 1-20	17, 18, 19
13	13:21-37	20, 21, 22
14	14: 1-26	23, 24, 25
15	14:27-53	26, 27
16	14:54-72	28, 29
17	15: 1-25	30, 31
18	15:26-47	32, 33, 34
		JOSH.
19	16	1, 2, 3
	LUKE	
20	1: 1-20	4, 5, 6
21	1:21-38	7, 8, 9
22	1:39-56	10, 11, 12
23	1:57-80	13, 14, 15
24	2: 1-24	16, 17, 18
25	2:25-52	19, 20, 21
26	3	22, 23, 24
		JUDG.
27	4: 1-30	1, 2, 3
28	4:31-44	4, 5, 6
29	5: 1-16	7, 8
30	5:17-39	9, 10
31	6: 1-26	11, 12

Appendix 4 (Continued)

APRIL

DATE	MORNING	EVENING
	LUKE	JUDG.
1	6:27-49	13, 14, 15
2	7: 1-30	16, 17, 18
3	7:31-50	19, 20, 21
		RUTH
4	8: 1-25	1, 2, 3, 4
		1 SAM.
5	8:26-56	1, 2, 3
6	9: 1-17	4, 5, 6
7	9:18-36	7, 8, 9
8	9:37-62	10, 11, 12
9	10: 1-24	13, 14
10	10:25-42	15, 16
11	11: 1-28	17, 18
12	11:29-54	19, 20, 21
13	12: 1-31	22, 23, 24
14	12:32-59	25, 26
15	13: 1-22	27, 28, 29
16	13:23-35	30, 31
		2 SAM.
17	14: 1-24	1, 2
18	14:25-35	3, 4, 5
19	15: 1-10	6, 7, 8
20	15:11-32	9, 10, 11
21	16	12, 13
22	17: 1-19	14, 15
23	17:20-37	16, 17, 18
24	18: 1-23	19, 20
25	18:24-43	21, 22
26	19: 1-27	23, 24
		1 KIN.
27	19:28-48	1, 2
28	20: 1-26	3, 4, 5
29	20:27-47	6, 7
30	21: 1-19	8, 9

MAY

DATE	MORNING	EVENING
	LUKE	1 KIN.
1	21:20-38	10, 11
2	22: 1-20	12, 13
3	22:21-46	14, 15
4	22:47-71	16, 17, 18
5	23: 1-25	19, 20
6	23:26-56	21, 22
		2 KIN.
7	24: 1-35	1, 2, 3
8	24:36-53	4, 5, 6
	JOHN	
9	1: 1-28	7, 8, 9
10	1:29-51	10, 11, 12
11	2	13, 14
12	3: 1-18	15, 16
13	3:19-38	17, 18
14	4: 1-30	19, 20, 21
15	4:31-54	22, 23
16	5: 1-24	24, 25
		1 CHR.
17	5:25-47	1, 2, 3
18	6: 1-21	4, 5, 6
19	6:22-44	7, 8, 9
20	6:45-71	10, 11, 12
21	7: 1-27	13, 14, 15
22	7:28-53	16, 17, 18
23	8: 1-27	19, 20, 21
24	8:28-59	22, 23, 24
25	9: 1-23	25, 26, 27
26	9:24-41	28, 29
		2 CHR.
27	10: 1-23	1, 2, 3
28	10:24-42	4, 5, 6
29	11: 1-29	7, 8, 9
30	11:30-57	10, 11, 12
31	12:1-26	13, 14

JUNE

DATE	MORNING	EVENING
	JOHN	2 CHR.
1	12:27-50	15, 16
2	13: 1-20	17, 18
3	13:21-38	19, 20
4	14	21, 22
5	15	23, 24
6	16	25, 26, 27
7	17	28, 29
8	18: 1-18	30, 31
9	18:19-40	32, 33
10	19: 1-22	34, 35, 36
		EZRA
11	19:23-42	1, 2
12	20	3, 4, 5
13	21	6, 7, 8
	ACTS	
14	1	9, 10
		NEH.
15	2: 1-21	1, 2, 3
16	2:22-47	4, 5, 6
17	3	7, 8, 9
18	4: 1-22	10, 11
19	4:23-37	12, 13
		ESTH.
20	5: 1-21	1, 2
21	5:22-42	3, 4, 5
22	6	6, 7, 8
23	7: 1-21	9, 10
		JOB
24	7:22-43	1, 2
25	7:44-60	3, 4
26	8: 1-25	5, 6, 7
27	8:26-40	8, 9, 10
28	9: 1-21	11, 12, 13
29	9:22-43	14, 15, 16
30	10:1-23	17, 18, 19

JULY

DATE	MORNING	EVENING
	ACTS	JOB
1	10:24–48	20, 21
2	11	22, 23, 24
3	12	25, 26, 27
4	13: 1–25	28, 29
5	13:26–52	30, 31
6	14	32, 33
7	15: 1–21	34, 35
8	15:22–41	36, 37
9	16: 1–21	38, 39, 40
10	16:22–40	41, 42
		PS.
11	17: 1–15	1, 2, 3
12	17:16–34	4, 5, 6
13	18	7, 8, 9
14	19: 1–20	10, 11, 12
15	19:21–41	13, 14, 15
16	20: 1–16	16, 17
17	20:17–38	18, 19
18	21: 1–17	20, 21, 22
19	21:18–40	23, 24, 25
20	22	26, 27, 28
21	23: 1–15	29, 30
22	23:16–35	31, 32
23	24	33, 34
24	25	35, 36
25	26	37, 38, 39
26	27: 1–26	40, 41, 42
27	27:27–44	43, 44, 45
28	28	46, 47, 48
	ROM.	
29	1	49, 50
30	2	51, 52, 53
31	3	54, 55, 56

AUGUST

DATE	MORNING	EVENING
	ROM.	PS.
1	4	57, 58, 59
2	5	60, 61, 62
3	6	63, 64, 65
4	7	66, 67
5	8: 1–21	68, 69
6	8:22–39	70, 71
7	9: 1–15	72, 73
8	9:16–33	74, 75, 76
9	10	77, 78
10	11: 1–18	79, 80
11	11:19–36	81, 82, 83
12	12	84, 85, 86
13	13	87, 88
14	14	89, 90
15	15: 1–13	91, 92, 93
16	15:14–33	94, 95, 96
17	16	97, 98, 99
	1 COR.	
18	1	100, 101, 102
19	2	103, 104
20	3	105, 106
21	4	107, 108, 109
22	5	110, 111, 112
23	6	113, 114, 115
24	7: 1–19	116, 117, 118
25	7:20–40	119: 1– 88
26	8	119: 89–176
27	9	120, 121, 122
28	10: 1–18	123, 124, 125
29	10:19–33	126, 127, 128
30	11: 1–16	129, 130, 131
31	11:17–34	132, 133, 134

SEPTEMBER

DATE	MORNING	EVENING
	1 COR.	PS.
1	12	135, 136
2	13	137, 138, 139
3	14: 1–20	140, 141, 142
4	14:21–40	143, 144, 145
5	15: 1–28	146, 147
6	15:29–58	148, 149, 150
		PROV.
7	16	1, 2
	2 COR.	
8	1	3, 4, 5
9	2	6, 7
10	3	8, 9
11	4	10, 11, 12
12	5	13, 14, 15
13	6	16, 17, 18
14	7	19, 20, 21
15	8	22, 23, 24
16	9	25, 26
17	10	27, 28, 29
18	11: 1–15	30, 31
		ECCL.
19	11:16–33	1, 2, 3
20	12	4, 5, 6
21	13	7, 8, 9
	GAL.	
22	1	10, 11, 12
		SONG
23	2	1, 2, 3
24	3	4, 5
25	4	6, 7, 8
		IS.
26	5	1, 2
27	6	3, 4
	EPH.	
28	1	5, 6
29	2	7, 8
30	3	9, 10

Appendix 4 (Continued)

OCTOBER

DATE	MORNING	EVENING
1	EPH. 4	IS. 11, 12, 13
2	5: 1–16	14, 15, 16
3	5:17–33	17, 18, 19
4	6	20, 21, 22
5	PHIL. 1	23, 24, 25
6	2	26, 27
7	3	28, 29
8	4	30, 31
9	COL. 1	32, 33
10	2	34, 35, 36
11	3	37, 38
12	4	39, 40
13	1 THESS. 1	41, 42
14	2	43, 44
15	3	45, 46
16	4	47, 48, 49
17	5	50, 51, 52
18	2 THESS. 1	53, 54, 55
19	2	56, 57, 58
20	3	59, 60, 61
21	1 TIM. 1	62, 63, 64
22	2	65, 66
23	3	JER. 1, 2
24	4	3, 4, 5
25	5	6, 7, 8
26	6	9, 10, 11
27	2 TIM. 1	12, 13, 14
28	2	15, 16, 17
29	3	18, 19
30	4	20, 21
31	TITUS 1	22, 23

NOVEMBER

DATE	MORNING	EVENING
1	TITUS 2	JER. 24, 25, 26
2	3	27, 28, 29
3	PHILEM. 1	30, 31
4	HEB. 1	32, 33
5	2	34, 35, 36
6	3	37, 38, 39
7	4	40, 41, 42
8	5	43, 44, 45
9	6	46, 47
10	7	48, 49
11	8	50
12	9	51, 52
13	10: 1–18	LAM. 1, 2
14	10:19–39	3, 4, 5
15	11: 1–19	EZEK. 1, 2
16	11:20–40	3, 4
17	12	5, 6, 7
18	13	8, 9, 10
19	JAMES 1	11, 12, 13
20	2	14, 15
21	3	16, 17
22	4	18, 19
23	5	20, 21
24	1 PET. 1	22, 23
25	2	24, 25, 26
26	3	27, 28, 29
27	4	30, 31, 32
28	5	33, 34
29	2 PET. 1	35, 36
30	2	37, 38, 39

DECEMBER

DATE	MORNING	EVENING
1	2 PET. 3	EZEK. 40, 41
2	1 JOHN 1	42, 43, 44
3	2	45, 46
4	3	47, 48
5	4	DAN. 1, 2
6	5	3, 4
7	2 JOHN 1	5, 6, 7
8	3 JOHN 1	8, 9, 10
9	JUDE 1	11, 12
10	REV. 1	HOS. 1, 2, 3, 4
11	2	5, 6, 7, 8
12	3	9, 10, 11
13	4	12, 13, 14
14	5	JOEL 1, 2, 3
15	6	AMOS 1, 2, 3
16	7	4, 5, 6
17	8	7, 8, 9
18	9	OBAD.
19	10	JON.
20	11	MIC. 1, 2, 3
21	12	4, 5
22	13	6, 7
23	14	NAH.
24	15	HAB.
25	16	ZEPH.
26	17	HAG.
27	18	ZECH. 1, 2, 3, 4
28	19	5, 6, 7, 8
29	20	9, 10, 11, 12
30	21	13, 14
31	22	MAL.

Notes

Chapter 2

1. William Walker, "What Wondrous Love Is This."
2. In some parts of American culture, accepting the free gift of salvation has at times been far too simplified, and as a result we've discouraged long, contemplative consideration of what it means to truly follow Jesus. With all the best intentions, some have created a subculture of very moral people, but ones who really don't have any true trust in Christ. If we truly are disciples of Jesus and we really love Him, we will trust Him and be primarily concerned with obeying what He asks of us.

Chapter 4

1. Leonard Ravenhill, *Why Revival Tarries* (Bloomington: Bethany House Publishers, 1959), 29.
2. "A Gift of a Bible," YouTube video, 5:11, posted by "beinzee," July 8, 2010, https://www.youtube.com/watch?v=6md638smQd8.
3. *Wait But Why* (blog) writers, "Why Generation Y Yuppies Are Unhappy," *The Blog* (from *Huffington Post*), September 15, 2013, http://www.huffingtonpost.com/wait-but-why/generation-y-unhappy_b_3930620.html.

Chapter 5

1. "The Theological Dictionary: Simul iustus et peccator," last modified September 21, 2012, accessed July 10, 2014, http://liberate.org/2012/09/21/the-theological-dictionary-simul-iustus-et-peccator/.
2. http://www.blueletterbible.org/lang/lexicon/lexicon.cfm?Strongs=G2588&t=NASB
3. "STRONGS NT 3809: παιδεία," *Thayer's Greek Lexicon*, Electronic Database. Copyright © 2002, 2003, 2006, 2011 by Biblesoft, Inc. All rights reserved. Used by permission, Biblesoft.com, on the Bible Hub website, accessed May 2,2 014, http://biblehub.com/greek/3809.htm.
4. John Stott in Letters of John, Tyndale New Testament Commentary Series, 1988; p.194

Chapter 6

1. Ted Dekker and Carl Medearis, *Tea with Hezbollah: Sitting at the Enemies' Table: Our Journey Through the Middle East* (New York: Doubleday Religion, 2010), 195.

Chapter 7

1. Edgar Allan Poe, "Alone," in *American Poetry: The Nineteenth Century*, vol. 1, *From Philip Freneau to Walt Whitman* (n.p.: Library of America, 1993), 522.
2. Some good reasons to leave a church are: the leadership is teaching contrary to Scripture and departing from orthodoxy; the leadership condones or is practicing sin unchecked; the members don't treat one another or the leadership in a Christlike manner; and so on. Some bad reasons to leave a church are because of personal preferences or comfort levels. The church doesn't exist to propagate consumerist Christianity.

Chapter 8

1. Robert Frost, *North of Boston* (New York: Henry Holt, 1917).
2. "Lexicon :: Strong's G1448 – *eggizō*," s.v., "ἐγγίζω," Blue Letter Bible (ESV), ACCESSED OCTOBER 31, 2013, http://www.blueletterbible.org/lang/lexicon/lexicon.cfm?Strongs=G1448&t=ESV.
3. W. A. Elwell and B. J. Beitzel, *Baker Encyclopedia of the Bible*, s.v. "shekinah" (Grand Rapids: Baker, 1988).
4. J. Swanson and O. Nave, *New Nave's Topical Bible*, s.v. "shekinah" (Oak Harbor, WA: Logos Research Systems, 1994).
5. K. C. Hanson and Douglas E. Oakman, *Palestine in the Time of Jesus: Social Structures and Social Conficts* (Minneapolis: Fortress, 1998), 132–34.
6. Ibid., 140–41.
7. Ibid., 139.
8. Ibid., 142.

Chapter 9

1. C. S. Lewis, *The Weight of Glory and Other Addresses* (New York: MacMillan, 1949).
2. C. S. Lewis, *The Problem of Pain* (New York: MacMillan, 1946).
3. Gary L. Thomas, *Sacred Pathways: Discover Your Soul's Path to God* (Grand Rapids: Zondervan, 2000).

4. *Strong's*, Blue Letter Bible, accessed May 5, 2014, http://www.blueletterbible.org/lang/lexicon/lexicon.cfm?Strongs=G3563&t=KJV&ss=1.
5. John Piper, *Desiring God: Meditations of a Christian Hedonist*, rev. ed. (Colorado Springs: Multnomah, 2011), 18.

Chapter 10

1. Elizabeth Barrett Browning (1806–1861), *Aurora Leigh* (London: J. Miller, 1864; Chicago: Academy Chicago Printers [Cassandra Editions], 1979).
2. "Current information on the scope and nature of child sexual abuse" *The Future of Children* 4, no. (1994): 31–53.
3. Many study Bibles offer insight into intertestamental period events, including the Greek and Roman occupations, the Maccabean revolt, and so on. You can also access the Holman Illustrated Bible Dictionary for free at www.mystudybible.com and look up the entry "Intertestamental History and Literature."

Chapter 11

1. J. R. R. Tolkien, *The Fellowship of the Ring: Being the First Part of The Lord of the Rings* (n.p.: George Allen & Unwin, 1954; New York: Houghton Mifflin Harcourt, 2012), 167.
2. K. C. Hanson and Douglas E. Oakman, *Palestine in the Time of Jesus: Social Structures and Social Conficts* (Minneapolis: Fortress, 1998), 50–51.
3. Carl Ludwig Wilibald Grimm and Christian Gottlob, *A Greek-English Lexicon of the New Testament: Being Grimm's Wilke's Clavis Novi Testamenti* (n.p.: Nabu Press, 2011).
4. C. S. Lewis, *The Last Battle* (New York: Collier Books, 1970).

SHARE THE INSCRIBED COLLECTION

EXPERIENCE THE BOOKS

Your friends can sample this book or any of our InScribed titles for FREE. Visit InScribedStudies.com and select any of our titles to learn how.

Know a church, ministry, or small group that would benefit from these readings? Contact your favorite bookseller or visit InScribedStudies.com/buy-in-bulk for bulk purchasing information.

CONNECT WITH THE AUTHORS

Do you want to get to know more about the author of this book or any of the authors in the InScribed Collection? Go online to InScribedStudies.com to see how you could meet them through a Google Hangout or connect with them through our InScribed Facebook.

JOIN IN THE CONVERSATION

 Like facebook.com/InScribedStudies and be the first to see new videos, discounts, and updates from the InScribed Studies team.

 Start following @InScribedStudy.

 Follow our author's boards @InScribedStudies.

 WWW.INSCRIBEDSTUDIES.COM

THOMAS NELSON
Since 1798